T0381120

LUCKY TO BE HERE

How to Discover Your Purpose, Live with Leadership, and Find Success

DR. PATRICK C. HORTON

BALBOA.PRESS

A DIVISION OF HAY HOUSE

Balboa Press books may be ordered through booksellers or by contacting:

Balboa Press
A Division of Hay House
1663 Liberty Drive
Bloomington, IN 47403
www.balboapress.com
844-682-1282

Because of the dynamic nature of the Internet, any web addresses or links contained in this book may have changed since publication and may no longer be valid. The views expressed in this work are solely those of the author and do not necessarily reflect the views of the publisher, and the publisher hereby disclaims any responsibility for them.

The author of this book does not dispense medical advice or prescribe the use of any technique as a form of treatment for physical, emotional, or medical problems without the advice of a physician, either directly or indirectly. The intent of the author is only to offer information of a general nature to help you in your quest for emotional and spiritual well-being. In the event you use any of the information in this book for yourself, which is your constitutional right, the author and the publisher assume no responsibility for your actions.

Any people depicted in stock imagery provided by Getty Images are models, and such images are being used for illustrative purposes only. Certain stock imagery © Getty Images.

Print information available on the last page.

ISBN: 979-8-7652-5157-7 (sc)
ISBN: 979-8-7652-5158-4 (e)

Library of Congress Control Number: 2024908069

Balboa Press rev. date: 05/06/2024

CONTENTS

Chapter 1

Find Your Purpose

I'd like to take you back to April 2003 when I found my purpose. And yes, the experience was as dramatic as that sentence.

The U.S. was just one month into Operation Iraqi Freedom, and I held an E-4 rank as a specialist, which is essentially an Army private with experience. (I'd been deployed previously to Kosovo for a peacekeeping mission.) My unit was tasked with taking the Baghdad Airport, and we were at a military checkpoint about 10 minutes away. It was hot and humid; I was outfitted in full battle gear, right down to my chemical mask, so I was that much more uncomfortable. But I was also locked in to the mission at hand. I had experience, I knew my mission, and I was ready to go.

Suddenly, an explosion propelled the gun barrel from an Iraqi tank into my back, breaking three of my ribs on impact. I was in and out of consciousness for the next several hours while I was medevacked to a military field hospital and placed on life support. Gradually, I regained consciousness and came face-to-face with what had happened—and what it meant.

As I lay there over the next 24 hours, I started asking myself, *If I died today, had I been someone my family would be proud of?*

Did I go talk to that girl I liked or was I too scared?

Had I been living as a leader or a follower?

Was I an honest and moral person at all times?

My answer every time was no. No! I had not lived up to my potential, and this could be it for me. I was only 23 years old, and I could be getting ready to take my last breath.

With this realization came an overwhelming horror as I pictured my mom and family dealing with the aftermath of my death. Lying on my hospital bed, I could see the Casualty Assistance Officer arriving with an American flag at my home in Vacaville, California, and notifying my mom that her only child had been killed in combat.

I also had one other thought. Although I'm not a religious man, a lot of my family is, and I do respect it. I said, "God, if you give me another chance, I promise I will make something of myself. I'm done half-assing life."

A doctor came in a few days later and told me that I had three broken ribs, potential lung damage, and torn tissue. He told me that my torso was starting to collapse and that I needed to breathe through a special tool whenever I was awake to keep my torso inflated and prevent pneumonia or death.

It was a sobering moment, but a joyful one too. My prayer had been answered, and I was granted another chance. The question was: What would I do with it?

* * *

The best decision I ever made was to join the military. I recommend it for anyone who doesn't have a clear path in life. And when I was 20 years old, I sure didn't.

Everything had fallen apart for me in my senior year in high school. Until then, I'd had a promising baseball career and was planning to attend Sacramento State University when I graduated. Trouble was, my GPA dropped to a 1.7 my senior year, which made me ineligible to play baseball and caused Sacramento State to rescind its offer to even attend school there. I became depressed and was really down at that point. I had no idea what I was going to do with my life outside of baseball.

I graduated high school anyway and started an IT degree at Heald College in Sacramento. I also got a job in retail with the help of my best friend's parents, but my performance was so poor I lost the job. I was flat broke. When people asked me what'd happened and I explained, I could see the disgust on their faces.

Eventually, I completed my associate degree in computer science. Having experienced so many ups and downs in life up to that point, I was in search of a change. I didn't know if that change would come from landing an IT job in Northern California, from venturing farther away in search of an IT opportunity, or from my newly researched option of joining the military.

One of the greatest gifts Heald College provided me was the ability to treat life decisions as if they were business decisions. Take the emotion out of it and look logically at the pros and cons of each move almost like a game of chess. What would be the return on investment if I got a regular IT job in Sacramento with no experience versus joining the military?

I can remember pulling out a legal pad and writing down the pros and cons of both options. With a local IT job, I reasoned, I'd be making roughly $15 to $18 an hour with few or no benefits. I'd be able to stay at home where I was comfortable. I was still picking up the pieces of my life after having made a lot of mistakes—would being in that environment help or hurt me? How would it affect my psyche and confidence living and working around so many people who'd seen my mistakes firsthand?

I hate to say it, but people can be unforgiving. They like to remind you over and over about your mistakes instead of just letting you move forward. Did I want to live in an environment where, even if I corrected my mistakes, everyone would remember and remind me of them?

I felt like part of the process of forgiving myself was sparing myself people's ridicule. As a vulnerable 20-year-old, I could easily spiral right back into depression. I wanted to go someplace where no one knew me, and where I would only be judged on my behavior moving forward.

If I were giving advice to someone who has had a public mishap, generally it wouldn't be to run away from their problems. It would be to stay, fight, and rebuild the trust they had lost. But there are times in life when a fresh start is necessary to free the soul from the weight of shame, regret, and the voices in your head. Almost like in the movies where the hero goes on a journey so that he can connect with his inner self and discover who he really is. For me, the military offered that pathway.

At 43, I now understand the value of leaving home and starting a new life. It's an opportunity to succeed, especially if you have people or habits holding you back at home. While attending Heald College, I found myself back in Sacramento's Oak Park neighborhood, where

I had a lot of family, including cousins who were attempting to start their adult lives. Most of my friends who had a purpose in life had moved away or were busy in college chasing their new life goals. I knew there was nothing good for me in Sacramento, because I couldn't seem to be a leader in my own life and stay out of compromising situations. Moving away would put some distance between me and the bad influences. It would force me to grow up and become a new man.

So, on September 10, 2000, I enlisted at an Army recruiting station in Sacramento. I received an $11,000 bonus, which I used to pay back my student loan. I was set to earn the equivalent of what I believed at the time was a $20/hour job. I would gain veteran status and, most importantly, I would acquire a brotherhood of friends and mentors that I desperately needed as a young, misguided man.

Of course, what I needed wasn't exactly what I was prepared for. The Army then was not the Army of today. And when I was shipped off to Fort Moore (formerly Fort Benning) in Georgia for basic training, I didn't know what I was in for.

* * *

About three to four weeks into boot camp, we had radio training. This was designed to teach new privates the phonetic alphabet, how to announce our identifier or call sign, how to transmit a message, how to state when our transmission was complete, and how to transition speaking privileges to the individual on the other end of the radio.

A typical correspondence would go something like: "Alpha 9, this is Charlie 9. I read you loud and clear. Over." Once "over" was stated, it would cue Alpha 9 that they could identify themselves and begin to transmit their message.

One fateful day, my head wasn't in the game for some reason. Within the last six months, I had lost both my grandmother and my best friend, Paul, who'd tragically drowned. I was operating in survival mode, just trying to make it to the next day. That particular day, maybe because basic training was starting to have its desired effect, I'd had enough. I wanted to give up on everything. Beaten down mentally, physically, and emotionally, I had nothing else to give the world.

It's not popular for men to talk too much about their state of mind or emotions as I'm about to do. At least, it's not popular in my community. Things are changing, and everyone has a different experience, but the way I grew up, men were supposed to suck it up, move on, and power through. If I'm being honest, I generally agree with this philosophy. If you dwell in your emotions as a soldier, you can get killed. If you dwell in them as a civilian, you can miss out on the job opportunity, the date, or the moment, because dithering can lead to low confidence.

But there are some days when, if you don't get it out, it will work against you.

When Paul died, I was in such shock that I didn't even cry at his funeral. I was dead inside. I simply stared ahead while I helped carry his casket to his final resting place. What I know now (and didn't know then) is that shock can make people behave this way only to reach a breaking point later on.

On that day of radio training, Drill Sergeant Copeland had been riding my butt trying to get the best out of me. He said, "Say the radio line, Private Horton."

I said the radio line, but I made a mistake.

"Wrong. Wrong, Private Horton. Say the radio line again."

Again, I attempted to say the radio line.

"Wrong. Wrong again, Private Horton." Raising his voice in anger, he shouted, "Say it again!"

I began to say the line, but before the third word came out, Drill Sergeant Copeland assumed an outright shouting stance in my face. As you can imagine, everyone stopped to see what was going on.

"Wrong again, Private Horton. Say it again."

I froze. I started to get dizzy, my mind was locking up on me, and I couldn't speak. I couldn't think. I'd taken all I could take. I tried to say the line again, and Drill Sergeant Copeland yelled out in response.

"Wrong f**king answer, Private Horton! Wrong f**king answer, Private Horton! Say it again!"

I broke down in an ocean of tears and, dizzy, I fell to one knee as the private behind me partially caught me. Drill Sergeant Copeland stopped the lesson. My squad leader took me to the side to cool off and calm down.

Back then, there were no stress cards to pull out when you started to lose your mind. You kept moving forward. Some of the instructors were Vietnam era or came from the 1990s Balkans conflict: They had seen real combat. Their job was to ensure that on the battlefield we maintained our composure and accomplished the mission. If we broke during war, not only could we get ourselves killed, we could get other service members killed as well.

As we moved on from radio training to other lesson stations, like rifle assembly, map navigation, chemical mask training, and squad fire maneuvering, I wondered if the other drill sergeants felt sorry for me. I made a few other mistakes that day, but the drill sergeants seemed to be a little more lenient with me.

By the time I got to my bunk that night, I was exhausted. Not many people spoke to me; they knew I was going through it. I fell asleep, exhausted. When I woke up the next morning, I felt like a bag of bricks was gone from my shoulders. My mind was clear. I felt like no matter what happened that day, there was nothing anyone could do to me that hadn't already been done.

I didn't know it then, but Drill Sergeant Copeland freed me from the constant weight of pain, anguish, and grief that had been ravaging my mind ever since I'd started to unravel in my senior year of high school. I was finally able to set those bad memories down and move forward with my life. Whatever spirit I had left inside of me finally broke free. From that day forward, I was essentially a new man.

* * *

In my opinion and experience (and others with different experiences will certainly hold their own opinions), military basic training is designed to break a man down to a child's level of acceptance. Then and only then can you rebuild him into a soldier and proud American citizen.

I was never the best soldier, but I was able to put together a pretty good career in the military after basic training. That training gave me direction and guidance, two precious commodities that college solidified. What I learned in those institutions set me up to keep pursuing, keep striving.

Ironically, the disciplined and structured life in the Army created the opportunity for me to be free. I think people often get freedom in life backward. They look at it as not going to school and not climbing the corporate ladder but taking on gigs and living according to whatever whim grips them. That's not freedom, though. That just enslaves you to low-wage jobs and an unstable life where you don't know where your next check (or your next job opportunity) is coming from.

Because I learned discipline, I put in the work and I advanced my career. I now have the freedom to travel and to retire when I want. Discipline in life gave me the freedom to make 10 times the choices about what I want both career-wise and life-wise.

*   *   *

If there's nothing else you take from this book, I hope you will embrace its one central lesson: Grab life's second chances.

Did I find my purpose only because almost dying forced me to wake up and consider what life really meant to me? Yes. And I believe it's a good idea to face head-on the fact that life is fragile and we are meant to find our purpose sooner rather than later. In the face of my mortality, I discovered the urgency to make every moment count, and I encourage you to do the same, preferably without the trauma of almost dying. Reflect on your own mortality. Recognize the value of your time on this earth. Embrace the reality and use that awareness as fuel to pursue your passions, dreams, and purpose with unwavering dedication.

Of course, my path wasn't a direct one to success. Before I became a college professor, company vice president, and entrepreneur, I encountered plenty of failures. Failure is an inevitable part of life, but it does not have to define us. I will share my experiences of hitting rock bottom and the arduous journey I undertook toward personal growth. I encourage you to view your own failures as stepping stones toward success, reminding yourself that setbacks are opportunities for self-reflection, learning, and resilience.

This is essentially what's known as a growth mindset. Life transformations require a mindset shift, from seeing challenges as insurmountable obstacles to opportunities for continual self-improvement. I developed a growth mindset by constantly seeking knowledge and pushing myself beyond my comfort zone to become the best person I could be. I hope you too adopt this mindset.

I also hope that, after reading this book, you choose to strive toward gratitude, toward improving your work ethic, and toward seizing opportunity when it presents itself. Gratitude is the foundation of a fulfilling life. I should know. I emerged with an immense sense of gratitude for the chance to make a difference not just in my life but in the lives of those around me.

Ultimately, I hope my story serves as a testament to the transformative power of making the most of life's second chances. You have the agency to shape your own destiny and create an extraordinary life filled with purpose, meaning, success, and adventure. But you have to be willing to put in the work. Luck favors the prepared, and success comes to those who are willing to put in the effort. That's why the people who work the hardest always seem to be the luckiest.

Through my story of failure, recovery, and transformation, I aim to inspire you to find your own second chances. The central message is clear: We are all fortunate to be here, and with hard work and determination we can shape our lives into something extraordinary.

My graduation from Army basic training in 2000 in Fort Moore, Georgia. I later received platoon leadership training, where I learned about being responsible for the lives of others and being accountable—lessons I carry with me to this day.

Combat training at Fort Stewart, Georgia. I would return one day to the post wounded both physically and mentally.

CHAPTER 2

YOUR BACKGROUND GUIDES YOU. IT DOESN'T DEFINE YOU

They say that to know where you're going, you have to know where you've been. To some extent this is true. Your family, your upbringing, your experiences—all these things shape you and your early opportunities.

In my case, I started out lucky—but not the way you might think. I wasn't born rich or powerful. I was simply born. How does that make me lucky? Well, my mother got pregnant with me when she was 18 and in a relationship with my father, who was 25. He wasn't interested in having kids. In fact, most people encouraged my mom to end the pregnancy. At the time, she was living in Memphis with my grandma, and something inside her wanted to keep me. So, she and my grandma decided to leave for California (where five of my grandma's other children were living) and not include my father in our lives.

I can only imagine how difficult a decision that was. In truth, it could've gone either way. But on March 17, 1980—St. Patrick's Day—she gave birth to me in Sacramento.

After I was born, it was just me and my mom living in the Oak Park neighborhood, but my mom knew it was a tough place for a kid to grow up. Gang violence, drugs, and unemployment plagued the area. She wanted to keep me close to family, but getting me out of Oak Park was her top priority in order to give me a real shot at life. So, when I was 4 years old we moved to Vacaville, a quiet city about 30 minutes away that back then was more farmland than big city. My mom found a job as a corrections officer at the California State Prison Solano. She was 22 years old, and it still amazes me how she had the wisdom so young to take a state job that would provide a full pension at 50.

Upon arriving in Vacaville, I met a few of the neighborhood kids who would become lifelong friends. The Whaley, Sobol, Jackson, and Shreve families took me in as their own. Out of the kindness of their hearts, they fed me, taught me life lessons, and let me spend the night at their homes.

Perhaps the most influential family to me outside of my own relatives was the Whaley family. Gary and Sheryl Whaley took me everywhere with them and their son, Sean, who is still my best friend. We went to waterparks, baseball games, and other activities I had never experienced before. You know, white people stuff.

Some of my fondest memories were when Gary let us 7-year-olds catch the wind as he drove through the country, and we stood out of the T-top roof of his red, 1980s Chevy Camaro. Or when Sheryl drove 90 miles an hour down I-80 with the T-tops off her 1991 RS Camaro. She'd be blasting AC/DC, Aerosmith, Motley Crew, Def

Leppard, and all that good 1980s and early '90s rock 'n' roll. I fell in love with that music because of them. It was a good time to be alive.

Like many kids growing up then, I was a latchkey kid just roaming the parks and neighborhoods for hours and hours on end. The only requirement was to be home by the time the streetlights came on. On the weekends, kids would leave the house around 9 or 10 a.m. and not come home until 7 or 8 at night. A simple, "Mom, I'm going to Sean's house and Cambridge Park," was enough.

We had no cell phones, pagers, or GPS devices on us. If your parents wanted to find you, they yelled your name from the front porch or drive around the block a few times until they found you. Or they called another parent to ask if you were at their house. If the parent didn't know, they sent their kid to go find you and report back. The community looked out for each other.

Of course, family looked out for each other too. My mom had a younger brother, my uncle Willie Horton, who filled the void of my father as best he could. He had his own family, but he spent as much time with me as possible. He taught me how to ride a bike and wash a car. He taught me a few basics about mechanics and how to generally conduct myself as a young man.

The other major family member in my life at that time was my grandmother. She'd walked me to school every day from the time I was in preschool until I was in sixth grade. One day when I was in fourth grade, I told my grandma she didn't have to walk me to school any longer, that I was big enough to make it around the corner on my own and walk with friends.

My grandmother replied that she walked me to school daily to make sure that I went because she'd only made it to third grade. She'd had to drop out to work in the fields of Mississippi and help watch her siblings while her parents went to work. When my grandmother told me this, I almost cried. I'd been so angry at the embarrassment of being seen walking to school with a 65-year-old woman that I didn't stop to think about how important it was to her to make sure I got an education since she hadn't been able to.

Growing up, I saw how Grandma took care of everyone in the family. She was the go-to person for a good meal, for a place to stay once she got her own place, and for wisdom when you needed someone to talk to. I watched her take care of her children, her brothers and sisters, and her community.

In this sense, Grandma gave me a foundation centered on generosity of spirit. Looking back, I recognize how fragile our family's survival felt and how my grandma's commitment to taking care of our family felt like more than just a good deed. It felt vital to our existence. I knew intrinsically that I had to grow up quickly to help with that responsibility. As I became more successful, it felt less like a choice and more like destiny: If I could help, I would.

*   *   *

My grandmother, Gladys Hoyt, was born in Mount Bayou, Mississippi, in August 1929. She grew up on a small farm in a family of sharecroppers. Later, she moved to Shelby County, also in Mississippi, to raise her 11 children.

My grandma couldn't read or write. In fact, the reason my last name is Horton and not Hoyt is because she couldn't read the birth certificate, and so her last four children have the last name Horton.

Life in Mississippi at that time wasn't kind to women like my grandma. She was only married once, to a man named AC Hoyt, but it didn't last. Her second relationship was an emotionally and

15

physically abusive one. According to family lore, the man had a girlfriend on the side who one day decided to kill my grandmother out of jealousy. The girlfriend showed up at the front door and shot my grandma once in the leg and once in the face (through her cheek) before fleeing.

My grandmother somehow made her way to her father's house, and her family got her to the hospital. Imagine 1940s medicine with a few gunshot wounds.

Eventually, the guy returned to reclaim my grandma. He showed up at the door of her family home and told my great-grandpa he wanted his woman back. My great-grandpa, standing in the doorway with his shotgun by his side, refused. An argument ensued during which the boyfriend tried to grab the shotgun and move my great-grandpa out of the way. In response, my great-grandpa shot him on the doorstep and killed him.

Later, the sheriff took my great-grandpa to the police station. But after hearing the story and seeing the state of my grandmother, the sheriff let my great-grandpa return home. From what I know, no charges were filed.

This all happened to my grandma before my mother was born. Had my grandmother been killed that day, my mother would have never been born. Shows you how lucky I am to be here.

* * *

Of course, I didn't always feel lucky growing up. And for all that my grandma wanted to make sure I got the education she didn't, I didn't always take advantage of it.

One thing I learned way too late is that, when it comes to childhood education, if you start behind, you finish behind. Because my mom worked as many overtime hours as she could to ensure we had enough money to pay the bills, I had a lot of unsupervised time on my hands. Instead of coming home and doing my homework, I would just go to the park and play sports or hang out with friends. I had every opportunity to do the right thing. I just chose not to.

As a result, I didn't learn everything I needed to learn in second grade, which made third grade that much harder. Fourth grade was even more difficult. By fifth grade, I found myself sitting in class, staring at the wall and praying that the teacher wouldn't call on me to read out loud because I knew I would be made fun of for sounding uneducated and being unable to pronounce most words that a fifth grader should know how to pronounce.

My reading and speech were so bad that I had speech therapy once a week in school from second through fifth grade. It's kind of funny, but as an adult I can see how this was advantageous. I was able to essentially get a private speech tutor who helped me learn how to pronounce words perfectly. That is one reason my diction is so good today.

While I could pronounce words well, I couldn't read very well. Back then, however, they did "social promotions" in school, meaning you'd keep moving up, grade by grade, to stay with your peers, even if your math and English skills didn't meet the standards. And mine didn't. While my classmates were reading at a fifth- or sixth-grade level by fifth grade, I was reading at a third-grade level.

My early education reminds me of a story I once heard about a man who planted two trees next to each other in his front lawn. He placed a stake next to each tree to help them grow straight and strong. Because the man was very busy, he hired others to take care of the trees. One day, he noticed one of the trees had started to grow sideways. The tree was still young and attached to the support structure, so all the man needed to do was take the time to go outside and reset the crooked tree so it could grow straight.

The man said, "I will get to it tomorrow." Days turned to weeks, and weeks turned to months but the man never found time to reset the young tree. After months of watching the tree grow sideways, the man finally decided to hire professional help to reset the tree. The professional came out, surveyed the tree, and said, "Sorry, sir. Because you let the tree grow crooked for so many months, there's no way to reset it. It will forever grow crooked."

The moral of this story is that as adults we often miss the opportunity to set the right roots for our children. We want to wait until they are 13, 14, or even older before we start to instill discipline and proper roots. But by that time it's too late.

In some ways, I was the crooked tree. One of my most vivid memories as a young teenager was coming home with a report card that had three F's, three D's, and one C. The man who would eventually become my stepfather, Robert Whitfield, took one look at my report card and said, "Damn, Patrick. What happened?"

Because I was so ashamed of my grades, all I could think to say was, "My teachers don't like me. That's why my grades are so bad."

Robert looked at me with a glint in his eye and said, "Oh okay. Man, that sucks. You seem like a pretty sharp kid. Doesn't make sense why your grades would be this low. Are you sure it's because your teachers don't like you? How much effort are you really putting into school? Is there anything you need from me?

"I see that you got a C in math. That class seems to be okay. Maybe going forward, you should put more effort into these other subjects.

Math and English are the most important subjects you will learn in school if you want to be successful in life."

He then said, "If you want to continue to play baseball, we have to get these grades up."

Now, baseball was the best thing I had going in my life. I'd been playing since I was 5, and it was a strong motivator for me.

Plus, the truth was I'd been lying through my teeth for years. I wasn't putting in the effort to get good grades, and Robert called me out on it. Remember a dozen paragraphs ago when I said, "If you start behind, you finish behind"? Because I hadn't learned all the lessons in fourth, fifth, and sixth grades, I found myself in seventh grade not doing most of the work because it had become too difficult by that point.

During those years, my mom did all she could. She was working 60 to 80 hours a week as a single mother trying to take care of me, my elderly grandmother, and a cousin who had come from Sacramento to live with us. Although she demonstrated an almost superhuman ability to handle everything, no one can do it all by herself. My mom caught most of the shenanigans I was into and corrected me, but when it came to school, I was able to manipulate the situation. I would get bad grades one quarter, and my mom would punish me. The next quarter, I would raise them dramatically. In her mind, she figured, "Okay, job done. Back to work." Another quarter later, my grades would drop again, and we would find ourselves going through this rope-a-dope over and over.

This is why I believe having two good parents in the home is so important and is the optimal situation. A strong male presence can deter or root out some of the behavior boys can get away with when they only have a mom in the home.

I wish I could say Robert's intervention was enough to reset my crooked tree. It wasn't. Eventually I'd get there. And who knows? Maybe his words were the seeds were what, at least in part, allowed me to flourish as an adult.

I also think that my early childhood instilled in me an independent or rebellious streak that doesn't want to conform to certain norms. In some aspects that has been my differentiator or strength. It gives me a kind of "I'm going to do life my way" attitude, which prevents me from following bad leaders off a cliff.

The flip side is I believe there is wisdom in tradition, and I've missed out on some of those benefits. I would be lying if I said not having a wife, children, and a home by the time I was 30 hadn't caused a certain level of sadness in my life. While some might say I was smart to have waited until my 40s, I still feel like I missed out on one of the main purposes of life, which is to have children. What's more, I feel like a nomad, always wandering, searching for life, adventure, and meaning. Could this be why, until I came to Florida, I hadn't lived in any single place for more than two years over the last two decades? Living a life of making the best choice you can with the information you find along your journey is a hell of a way to live.

These challenges have ultimately contributed to my growth. I'm not yet done with life. There is more to accomplish, more to learn, and more to contribute to the world. My past, with its ups and downs, is a powerful asset when it comes to making decisions and solving problems. And I believe that our destiny is determined not by where we started in life but in how we choose to navigate our journeys ahead. Our background can be our strength if we know how to grow skills and wisdom from it.

* * *

Growing up is inextricably tied to school, and school is much more than grades and classes. As everyone knows, one of the biggest factors of our school experience is our social experience. I made some great friends during that period of my life, but I also learned the valuable lesson of how and when to stand up for myself.

When I was a kid, I got the same bullying that kids likely get today, but there was no internet, so it stopped when you got home. I can remember the bullying as if it happened yesterday. *You're too dark. Your hair is nappy. Your clothes are horrible.*

I never understood why kids engaged in this type of behavior. There is no greater scum on this earth than someone who makes fun of others for personal gain. Spare me the psychological reasons pertaining to past trauma. Maybe that's sometimes true, but to hell with it. The ownership of this behavior needs to be on the kids perpetrating it and their parents who don't teach them better. The true victim is the kid at the end of the bullying. I am a protector, and I tried to shield other kids from being bullied when I was younger.

One day I was the one who needed protecting. I was in seventh grade, riding the bus home from school. An eighth grader on the bus started trash-talking and making fun of me. This kid was known to everyone in the neighborhood as someone who got in a public fight at least once a month.

That fateful day the bully knocked my books on the bus floor and called me a vulgarity in front of everyone on the bus. He was going on with, "Who do you think you are? Do you think you're special? I should whip your ass when we get off this bus."

I have to admit I was scared, but I held my composure and didn't flinch. I just looked back at him with a frown and kept my mouth shut, trying to not engage. He had a few good laughs with his friends on the bus at that.

The wild thing was that none of the kids got off at their usual stops. By the time we got to my stop there would normally be about 15 kids left on the bus. That day there were 30 kids, and when we reached my stop, they all—and I mean every last kid—got off the bus.

By the time I realized what had happened, I looked back and the bus driver sped off. I was thinking, "That driver just left me to get jumped by the entire city block."

I had my core group of friends there, and they had my back. Then I remembered that Uncle Willie was supposed to be at my house when I got home so we could go to the movies, and the bus stop was almost within sight of my house. S**T.

I started to walk in the direction of my home when I heard the bully scream, "You f**king p***y!"

I turned and looked at the bully, who was across the street. I yelled, "What the hell is your problem?"

He screamed, "Shut the f**k up."

I'd had enough. "Well, what's up then!?"

This was what he had been waiting for. He wanted to push my buttons to the point where he could justify starting the fight. He quickly crossed the street and threw a haymaker punch. He missed. I grabbed him, pushed him against a fence and said, "I don't want to fight you." He was struggling to get free and kept cursing and talking trash. I threw him back and said again, "I don't want to fight you."

22

He walked in my direction and threw another haymaker, missing again. I grabbed him and held him against the fence. After what felt like an eternity, I threw him off and said, "I'm not playing with you. Back off."

As I walked backward, he came straight at me.

I yelled, "F**k this," reached back, and threw the hardest Mike Tyson overhand right I could muster. My fist connected with his temple, and he fell to the ground.

I could hear every kid screaming, "OHHHHHHHHHH! He just got knocked out cold. Damn!"

When I saw the bully on the ground, my stomach bottomed out. I thought I had killed him. But he staggered up, gathered his things, delivered a few bad parting insults and walked away.

I started walking home with my friend Paul. I was scratched up, and my shirt was ripped. We were two doors down from my house when, of course, here comes Uncle Willie's baby blue '85 Ford Ranger pulling into my driveway. I had no time to hide. Uncle Willie took one look at me before asking, "Boy, what happened to you?"

There was no lying to Uncle Willie, who was the size and build of Mike Tyson. So I said, "I just got into a fight."

At that point Paul was like, "See ya, Pat!"

Uncle Willie asked, "Where does he live?"

"Up the street."

"Did you start it?"

"No, sir."

"Did you win?"

"Yes, sir."

"Good," he replied. "Now get in the car. We are going over to his house to speak with his parents."

We drove around the corner to the bully's house, and Uncle Willie knocked on the door. The bully's father answered, and my uncle said, "Hello, sir. My nephew just came home, and I saw his shirt all ripped up. He let me know that he had been in a fight with your son."

The bully's father said, "Yeah, he's in here now putting ice on his eye."

Uncle Willie said, "Yeah, all is good. I think they both have learned their lesson, and I want to make sure that whatever happened ends here and doesn't continue tomorrow when they go to school."

The bully's father agreed, and they shook hands and closed the door. On our way home, Uncle Willie told me that fighting was never a good answer, but if you have to protect yourself, that is what you have to do.

"Never let anyone push you around," he said. "Only fight if you don't have another option. And I'd better not hear anything else about you fighting this guy again. You understand?"

I said, "Yes, sir!"

After that day, and almost until I graduated high school, I never had another fight at school. In fact, it was known that if you messed with Patrick, you might get knocked out. It's crazy how school politics work.

I also learned something about myself that day. When I stood up to the bully, I recognized the importance of using courage and strength to confront adversity. I also discovered another aspect of my identity: that of a protector and fighter who would not be overrun in life.

I began to view life's obstacles as battles that demanded resilience, adaptability, and a refusal to back down. This mindset shaped me into the determined and resilient individual I am today, ready to tackle any challenge that comes my way.

* * *

Between school, friends, and family, my early life was busy and full. It was also a time when I discovered my talent and passion for baseball.

Because my mom worked a lot and my dad was not in my life, I was a young man in need of mentorship and some activity. My mom signed me up for T-ball when I was 5 years old. From there, I found baseball, which would become my salvation. It was one thing I was good at and that kept me out of trouble.

My dream as a young man was to play professional baseball. I used to imagine myself starting in center field for the San Francisco Giants. As a kid in the '80s and '90s, I used to watch Atlanta Braves baseball every day because it aired on TBS daily around the country. I used to love Dave Justice, Fred McGriff, Chipper Jones, and the four-headed monster pitching staff of Greg Maddux, Tom Glavine, John Smoltz, and Steve Avery.

By 1996 I was living my own dream as a sophomore at Will C. Wood High School in Vacaville, playing baseball on the junior varsity team. I and three other players (Ricky, Aaron, and John) were local all-stars leading the JV team to a record year. Our varsity team, however, was 0-12. Seeing how the four of us were having so much success on the JV team, the varsity baseball coach pulled us into a room and said, "Gentlemen, I would like to pull the four of you up to varsity to start in the next game."

We were flattered and beyond excited to play varsity as sophomores. We practiced with the team and could see instantly that we would make a positive impact. I was in center field, Ricky was our ace pitcher and also played right field, Aaron was at shortstop, and John was at third base.

For my first varsity game, I was hitting in the leadoff spot. As the game was starting, this big lefty walked to the mound. He was sizable, but I noticed in warmups he wasn't throwing very hard. Maybe 70 to 75 mph tops. I was riding high having just been promoted to varsity and hitting leadoff in my first game. I was on top of the world. The catcher threw down to second base to wrap up warmups.

This was my moment. My dream. I was on varsity. Would I hit a home run in my first at bat? Would I hit a double or single or hit something hard and get out? I needed to make a mark, and this was my chance. "Let's do this," I said to myself. Staring at the pitcher, I thought, "Serve that weak s**t up, 'cause I'm about to take you for a ride."

The pitcher started from the windup and went into his left-handed throwing motion. He reared back and threw. He threw a 96-mph fastball down the middle of the plate, and I froze!

The ball exploded into the catcher's mitt, and I thought, *WTF was that?* He threw so hard I didn't even see the ball leave his hand or cross the plate.

In between pitches, I took my left foot out of the batter's box and looked at my third-base coach and mumbled loud enough for him to hear, "This is varsity? Pfft, I don't need this s**t!"

Before I knew it, the pitcher threw strike two at 95 mph, then strike three, also at 95 mph with me swinging. On my way back to the dugout, my head coach and third-base coach said, "Don't worry, Patrick. Everyone is going to strike out." Everyone laughed. The pitcher was none other than CC Sabathia, who went on to the play 19 seasons of Major League Baseball with the Cleveland Indians, Milwaukee Brewers and New York Yankees.

As you can imagine, we lost as CC gave up two hits in five innings. He also hit a 400-foot home run to right field for our pleasure. I was playing against greatness in the making. CC was 6'7" and 300 pounds. He played football, he played on the state champion Vallejo High School basketball team, and he was an All-American baseball player.

I would go on to play against CC for the next three years in high school. I was no CC, but in 1998 I was one of the top high school baseball players in California. I was throwing 90 mph by my senior year with a batting average of .450 and four home runs. I was a Sacramento County Optimist All-Star, MEL First Team All League (second to only CC Sabathia), and a Solano County All-Star. I held a host of other batting titles for my school and in the area.

Vacaville baseball was full of legends who never made it because we never got a look. We played between San Francisco and Sacramento. The major colleges were in Sacramento and the Bay Area. We used to beat up on those teams from the Bay Area and Sacramento year-round. When I started going to the prestigious All-Star games, the players I met would tell me they had full-ride scholarships to the University of San Francisco, Sacramento State, USC, UCLA, UC Davis, and so on. Our players from Vacaville were just as good if not better, but we were smack in the middle of cow town. (*Vacaville* literally means "cow town" in Spanish.) Unless you had obvious superhuman talent like CC did, you didn't get a look from major colleges.

In my case, I also had myself to blame. My dreams of baseball greatness took a detour during my senior year. I began to lose focus on what was important to me, and I let my grades drop below a 2.0 GPA. This made me ineligible to play until I appealed and got back on the field. But that was the beginning of the end. I'd played 40 to 60 games every summer since I was 13. That intense load, on top of the high school season, led to burnout by the time I was 18.

One of my life's regrets is that I lost the passion for baseball and didn't play in college. I could handle failing and not making it to the pros. The fact that I spent so much of my life honing the craft of baseball and didn't even give myself a shot at the next level still breaks my heart.

Eventually, I found my way to the military, college, and success. It worked out. Although I wish I could say I had planned it that way all along, that wasn't the case. Sometimes life throws you a curveball (or a 95 mph CC Sabathia fastball). Sometimes you throw yourself under the bus and sabotage your hopes and dreams with bad decisions. Whatever your situation, life rarely follows a planned trajectory. What matters more than a plan is resilience. If you can push through, learn from your mistakes, and continue to strive for your dream, you will find happiness.

It's okay to not have everything figured out at the beginning. In fact, it's unpredictability that allows us to grow, evolve, and discover our true passions, strengths, and purpose.

* * *

The sooner you realize this, the better. Because, as my cousin Leroy proves, it's not enough to let your circumstances carry you through life.

Of all my male cousins, Leroy was my favorite. He was about five years older than me, and the big brother I never had. In an effort to keep him out of trouble, he moved to Vacaville around the time he was a junior in high school.

Leroy had legitimate college basketball talent. Watching him play was like watching art in motion. He had creative ball-handling skills, he could shoot, and he could dunk. No wonder Solano Community College was recruiting him to play point guard.

Leroy was also, no question, one of the best hip-hop dancers I had ever seen. Saturday mornings at my place would consist of waking up by 9 to do chores and watch Leroy breakdance all over the house while vacuuming and doing dishes to Kid 'n Play jams. He would walk up to me, grab my arm and start the breakdance snake rotation. It was crazy how much life he had in him.

Leroy was also a ladies' man. In the morning, I would see women's shoes in the living room and walk up next to his door to see if I could hear anyone whispering. Leroy didn't have a car, but I would see cute high school and college girls come by to pick him up and take him around.

Leroy was also a nice dresser. He had a collection of colorful, ironed, button-up shirts lined up in his closet. Although they were a little big for me, he used to let me wear them to my junior high dances so that I looked sharp. I used to get super excited when he would take me into his closet and help me pick out a shirt. He'd say, "Cuz, we got to get you fresh for the school dance. You gonna be up there lookin' right!"

Like many high school kids, Leroy and his friends dabbled with alcohol and marijuana. When Leroy graduated high school, he started the process of applying to the state prison where my mom worked. This would have been an amazing opportunity for him. He would have had the security of a state job and a salary that would let him start an independent life.

After Leroy passed the written exam, he was asked if he had ever used drugs. I know I'm supposed to say you should always tell the truth because it's the right thing to do. But if you don't have a criminal record and you are smart about your exposure, no one can prove anything. Why chance disqualifying yourself from a life-changing career opportunity?

Leroy told the truth. As a result, his application was thrown out and he was disqualified from state employment.

When a man doesn't have a purpose, he sometimes goes to a dark place. Although Leroy's personality was upbeat, I could tell that he'd started to hang out more, drink more, and smoke weed more. He was searching for answers.

One day Leroy pulled me aside and said, "Hey, Cuz, sorry to tell you this, but I'm moving to Washington state." He'd found what I think was a "Deadliest Catch" type of job that was well paid and involved going out to sea to hunt for crab and fish. Leroy told me when he was leaving and then packed up for his adventure.

I was in eighth grade. After Leroy left, I did not hear from him or have any knowledge of his whereabouts for five years. It was as if he disappeared off the face of the earth, and I was heartbroken. When Leroy moved out, I got his room in the house. I would sit by the window and just stare out of it, wondering where he was. Was he okay? Was he happy? Did he find love and happiness?

I hoped that one day the phone would ring, and he would be on the other end to tell me about all the fun he was having traveling the world. The call never came.

By the time I was out of high school and going through my own challenges trying to discover who I was as a man, Leroy resurfaced. He had completely changed.

For five years, Leroy had traveled through the Northwest and became addicted to crystal meth, alcohol, cocaine, and other drugs. His subsequent health complications, including heart issues and the onset of blindness, made him eligible to receive a disability check from the state. He quietly settled in Sacramento and worked a construction job.

We attempted to reconnect, but it was just never the same. I could tell that life had done a number on him and that his mental and physical faculties had eroded. Drugs had ravaged his mind.

What no one wants to admit is that life consequences are different for people who have money and those who don't. If you're a wealthy kid, you can afford to have a drug binge or two, and your family structure will be there to help you pick up the pieces. When you are less financially stable, the world is less forgiving. You mess up, get a drug habit, get into a little trouble, and your whole life can be irredeemable.

Leroy passed away when he was about 50 years old. If I am correct, I think his heart gave out, which is almost poetic: A person with one of the biggest hearts I have ever seen moved on to the next life because his heart in this life simply couldn't take anymore.

* * *

If I were doing an impartial case study, this is what I would report to you. Out of the seven boys I grew up with in my family, all of them either spent 10-plus years in and out of jail and prison or struggled to succeed in life. They were smarter, were better looking, and had more charisma and personality than I did. The only difference was that I grew up in the suburbs and they grew up in the inner city when Oak Park had serious challenges with gangs, drugs, crime, and poverty.

I'm here to tell you your environment and the influences that shape you play an incredibly important role in the opportunities you have for success. I spent my youth playing sports, attending a suburban school, and getting into minimal trouble. My mom told me how smart I was. She told me that I was a handsome young man and that I could do anything I put my mind to. Such affirmation gave me the foundation that I carry with me today and that enabled me to achieve the things that I have. I've never heard a "You can't do that." Even if she privately thought I was crazy for trying something and knew it probably wouldn't work out, she gave me the confidence to push beyond my limitations. Nine times out of 10, I'd accomplish the goal.

My cousins, on the other hand, were exposed to so much more adult-level crime, violence, danger, promiscuity, and the other challenges that accompany fighting for life in an inner city.

Maybe the biggest disadvantage they had, however, was not recognizing their own agency. Although a person's past, upbringing, and circumstances can present certain challenges, they do not necessarily define one's future. In facing my own life challenges, I've learned that the way to overcome them is through hard work and placing myself in the right environment to achieve success.

You can't be afraid to fail in life. What's more, you need to appreciate the life you have. That doesn't mean it's all sunshine and rainbows. I've failed more times than I can count: exams, friendships, work projects, women, and a million other ways. But what sticks with me to this day aren't my failures. They're my regrets. They're the things I was too scared to try. The outside influences that I allowed to become my own. I regret not attempting to play pro baseball after pouring all of my energy into it. I wake up every day wondering what could have been. And I will never let that happen again. Failure is a part of life; we just have to be smart and learn from our experiences and the mentors who grace us with their tutelage.

If you take nothing else from this chapter, please take the wisdom that we should attack life aggressively from the beginning. I repeat: Don't be afraid to fail. Otherwise, your soul will carry the burden of unfulfilled aspirations. You have the ability to rise above your circumstances if you have self-awareness and an eye for opportunity.

I told you I was lucky. And luck favors the prepared.

**My mother, Bernice Whitfield, my number-
one supporter. My luck in life began with her
decision as a teenager to give birth to me.**

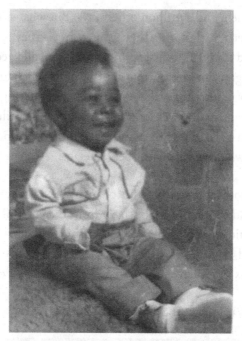

My first few years were in a tough neighborhood in Sacramento, but my mother soon moved us to Vacaville, California, for a better environment to grow up in.

My cousin Leroy was like a big brother to me. I idolized him, but ultimately our lives took different paths.

With my high school baseball coaches in
1998. The sport was my passion.

ALL-REGION BASEBALL

MOST VALUABLE PLAYER: C.C. SABATHIA Vallejo

POSITION	NAME	SCHOOL	YE
Pitcher	Josh Garcia	Vanden	1
Catcher	David Bernstine	Vallejo	1
Infielder	Joe Gevas	St. Pat's	1
Infielder	Keith Mendonsa	Benicia	1
Infielder	Kurt Mendonsa	Benicia	1
Infielder	Sean O'Brien	Vacaville	1
Infielder	Lalo Calvo	Vanden	1
Utility	Damien Lopez	St. Pat's	1
Outfielder	Kevin Conyers	Benicia	1
Outfielder	Pat Horton	Wood	1
Outfielder	Otis Brown	Vallejo	1

I was among the top players in my region of California and
even faced CC Sabathia. One of my regrets is that I didn't
take my athletic talent as far as I could after high school.

Chapter 3

Change Maker

Going after what you want in life is one thing. Knowing when you need to change your goals, your environment, or even yourself to get it? Well, that's something else altogether.

I should know. My journey began with facing the loss of an opportunity to play college baseball at Sacramento State. This setback forced me to seek a new path by joining the military, which provided the structure and discipline I didn't know I needed to reshape my life. Over three tours of duty, I had a close call with death that forced me to confront my mortality and reassess my goals and priorities.

Those were some of the big events that required change from me, but there were also smaller shifts along the way. Using these little but frequent opportunities to recalibrate kept me on the bigger path toward success.

In the fall of 2003, for example, everyone in my unit came home to Fort Stewart in Georgia, but not everyone reintegrated well. Some soldiers who were squared-away troops before combat (the ones who showed up on time, did their jobs well, went home, and did it all over again the next day) ended up going off the deep end. Some went on drug binges, others had issues with alcohol, and some became violent, getting into fight after fight in downtown Savannah. There were reports of troops having domestic violence issues.

Some behavior was directly related to being in combat, and some was related to coming home to find their lives in shambles. Troops found that wives and girlfriends had left them, cheated on them, spent all their money, or embarrassed them. Every possible situation you could think of happened.

The command did the best it could through counseling, training, and family events, but the number of divorces on base was staggering. I don't know the stats, but it seemed as if between 50% and 75% of married couples started breaking up. It felt like the people who didn't have a good family support structure faced the most issues when we returned home.

I didn't have a wife, but I did have my own challenges. I came to Fort Stewart injured both physically and mentally. I'd been wounded in combat, but I'd also experienced the trauma of war in general and of being missing in action during one particular event.

*   *   *

During Operation Iraqi Freedom, I was part of an infantry battalion out of Fort Stewart that arrived in Iraq. We were a month into the invasion, and, as the communication chief, I was assigned to drive a big rig full of equipment from both the communication and medical departments.

Because my load was so heavy and we were driving in soft sand in southern Iraq, my vehicle kept getting stuck. My unit had to use tow trucks and dedicated tanks to pull my truck out of the sand. After this happened four or five times, my commanding officer told me, "Horton, we have to meet our objective and your vehicle keeps getting stuck because it's too heavy. We need to move forward without you. The unit to our rear will pick you up." I agreed and waited until the next unit arrived.

As I began moving with another military company on our march to Baghdad, my vehicle continued to get stuck. So, the second company I was with decided to leave me for the following unit. This happened three more times until no more units came to pick me up. It was me and a new first lieutenant who had just graduated college. We had no radio, no cell phone, no map, and no GPS device, and we didn't know when the next military unit was coming. Oh, and no one knew where we were. We were officially MIA.

All I could think of as the leader in the vehicle was that we had to continue to drive in the direction of Baghdad and hope that we'd come across another U.S. military unit.

Around day two of being missing, the exhaustion that was part and parcel of war began to catch up with me. I can remember driving through the desert, lost and delirious with fatigue to the point where I'd start to fall asleep at the wheel. I'd pull over to rest and wake up disoriented, unsure of where I was or what I was supposed to be doing. It would take several moments before I'd remember, "Oh yeah, I'm at war in Iraq, and I'm missing in action." I had to keep driving to find a friendly unit.

We were MIA for three days. Not to get too deep into the enemy contacts we encountered, but at one point I was driving, shifting gears, taking enemy fire, and returning fire with my M-16 out the driver's window. I had my night-vision goggles on so I could see while driving as fast as I could to escape enemy engagement.

On the third day and after driving for hours, we ran into a random military tactical operations center stationed at the Karbala Gap, and I was able to radio my unit and link back up with them close to Baghdad.

Just days later I would be injured in combat, which set off another chain of events that would haunt me when I came home. Like many soldiers, I had nightmares of battle. I couldn't remember everything about being blown up, but my dreams would reveal details that I'd puzzle over, wondering if they were real or imagined. I could see the dead bodies; I could hear the Warthog airplanes and the distinct sound they made when dropping artillery. If I went to sleep and heard thunder, I would wake up panicked, thinking it was enemy fire. I'd scramble to find my M-16, being attached to it for months in Iraq, and then panic again because it wasn't there.

Being awake wasn't much better. I hated being in large crowds because I felt exposed, as if someone could sneak up on me at any moment. When I drove and saw reckless drivers, I got road rage. I wanted to strangle people for being inconsiderate.

It wasn't long before I began to drink to cope. My wakeup call came from my roommate, Duwane, when we were living at Fort Stewart. He came home one day and said, "Man, Patrick. You've been drinking a lot. I always see you coming from the liquor store, or I see all of the beer come and go in the refrigerator. Are you good? I can't drink with you like this every night, because I have to work in the morning."

I was just 23 years old, but I was putting away, at minimum, a 12-pack of Heineken every day. This was a lot for me; I'd never drunk like that before. And I could feel it. I had physical fitness training every morning, and while I wouldn't show up drunk, I would sometimes be buzzed or just not 100% because I'd been drinking so much the night before.

After a few weeks, I had to check myself. *What am I doing?* I started seeing how much money I was spending on alcohol, how I was drinking alone most of the time, and how Duwane was starting to notice. Plus, I felt awful. So, I made a change. I didn't go cold turkey, but I made a rule that I would no longer drink on weekdays and I would limit myself to three or four drinks on weekends. That way, I would feel better during morning training and, if nothing else, I wouldn't have to feel embarrassed by my roommate looking at me as if I had a drinking problem.

* * *

Drinking was only part of it. As with other soldiers who had trouble adjusting to civilian life, my difficulties shifted and changed depending on where I was and what I was doing. To find my way, I needed both self-discipline and family support.

When I got my 30 days of free leave after being injured in combat, I went back to Vacaville to stay with my parents. Most friends and family just wanted to make sure I was okay and hear my story about what had happened. All I could tell them at the time was what I thought had happened: I had, after all, been unconscious for most of the ordeal.

Well, they were impressed even with that partial recounting. I have never been bought more drinks or given more free dinners than when I first arrived home from the war. Physically, I was still in bad shape and recovering from three broken ribs. Mentally, I just wanted to lay low. I'd seen so much death and destruction that I didn't want to bring any additional attention to myself as I tried to figure out who I was.

Family and friends didn't listen. Everywhere I went, they were like, "Hey, this is my cousin [or friend] Patrick! He just got back from the war where he got blown up." Every single bar and restaurant was like, "Hey, drinks are on us, dinner is on us."

And if the restaurants and bars didn't offer to pay, a customer would walk over, thank me for my service, and buy me a drink or two. It was like a World War II movie. You come home and everyone thanks you for fighting for their freedom.

It really humbled me. As a soldier, I had been caught up in the day-to-day survival of going to war and making sure I was where I needed to be. I didn't have time to think of what I was even really doing. But the outpouring of love and support from friends and family helped me transition back into normal life.

Knowing what I know now, the worst thing I could have done was to be alone to stew in my own thoughts. Every time I went home to California between 2003 and 2006, my friends and family would stop what they were doing and make it a point to come see me. We would go out for drinks, have barbecues, and just hang out and talk for hours. I believe the community support helped me navigate the change successfully from soldier to civilian.

* * *

When I wasn't in California I was in Georgia. I was still in the Army, so I had sustainable income for the first time in my life, and while I wasn't rich, I could afford to go on a date, drive a nice car, and live a good life.

I also liked looking good, so every three or four days, I was at Nu-Image Barber & Beauty Salon getting a razor-edge temple taper from one of the best barbers in Georgia: my roommate, best friend, and mentor, Duwane. He was in his late 20s at the time with two daughters, and he would sprinkle game and wisdom on me every time I was in his barber's chair.

In Black culture, there was no bigger influence outside of New York City than Atlanta. I was going to Def Poetry Night, hanging out at the hair show in Atlanta with VIP access to certain events, and running with some of the most sought-after entertainment people in the Savannah region. I loved living in Georgia.

I ended up renting a room from Duwane for two years while I was recovering and figuring out my next steps. He taught me so much about what it meant to be a stand-up African American man in the 2000s. Long gone were the days of being a hoodlum. We were on a mission to improve our money, game, frame, and status. It was an amazing time to be alive.

I lived in Hinesville, just outside of Fort Stewart, with Duwane until April 2006, when I exited the Army. Duwane helped me make the decision to take my first job as a contractor in Baghdad. He recognized that the opportunity to sign on as a $135,000-a-year, tax-free contractor right out of the military was an opportunity to set myself up for success no matter what I decided to do next. As he pointed out, I had been a soldier doing raids in downtown Baghdad for $35,000 a year. If I were going to live a dangerous life, I may as well go back and take a $100,000 raise.

Duwane acquired some of his wisdom because he'd had his first daughter when he was 22 years old. He had to grow up fast to support his family, both when he was married and after he was divorced with two kids. Duwane had a lot of mentors, like his father, his grandfather, and a wise Southern gentlemen who had found success. When I had a difficult situation, I could simply ask Duwane. He was an intellectual who enjoyed thinking two levels deep on life fulfillment and success.

* * *

My path to working as a contractor was hard-won. Between 2001 and 2005, I did three combat tours, and I was exhausted. I'd go to war only to come back to Fort Stewart to train for war. By 2005, I was serving at Forward Operating Base Falcon in Iraq, and I knew it would be my last combat tour as a soldier.

Once that tour ended, I was going through out-processing at Fort Stewart when my signal officer at the time, Captain Christadore, called me into his office. "Sergeant Horton," he said, "there is a company named Proactive Communications, which is a government contractor. They just offered me a job to go overseas as a satellite systems installer. I'm not interested in taking the job, but if you are, I can make a recommendation."

I immediately said yes. Back in 2001, when I was in the early stages of my Army career, I was stationed at Camp Monteith in Gnjilane, Kosovo, on a peacekeeping mission. While there, I came into contact with several Microsoft help desk contractors who were making six figures a year working to support the U.S. Army. As soon as I met them, I knew I wanted to become a contractor overseas one day. They made big salaries, and I knew a role like that would help jump-start my civilian career.

Proactive was based outside of Fort Hood in Killeen, Texas. After I finished out-processing, I packed up my 2000 F-150 and drove from Georgia to California. On my way, I stopped in Killeen to take the interview with Proactive. By the time I arrived home in Vacaville, I had an offer letter in my inbox.

Before I knew it, I was back in Baghdad, this time as a combat zone forward support representative satellite systems installer living in the International Zone across the street from the Iraqi Minister of Defense. It was an exciting move. There I was, fresh out of the military making six figures and traveling extensively to perform satellite system installations in locations like Fallujah, Ramadi, Anbar Province, Balad, Tikrit, Tal Afar, Baghdad, and Mosul.

Without question, this was the most dangerous job I'd ever had. Baghdad in 2006 was much more dangerous than even my days working at FOB Falcon. From what I recall, this was the start (or at least the escalation) of the Sunni and Shia death squads going into neighborhoods and kidnapping or killing people. Attacks on military bases were up that year. I didn't take cabs; I took Black Hawk and Chinook helicopters daily to various locations where I would install satellite systems and local area networks.

To give you an idea of what this looked like, I can recall being sent to the Ramadi air base to install satellite systems for the Ramadi police station and the U.S. Marine Corps at Camp Blue Diamond. I remember driving out to the police station thinking it looked like a scene from *Saving Private Ryan*. As we drove through town, every building was riddled with bullets. It was eerily quiet: We knew there were snipers, roadside bombs, and enemy combatants hidden throughout the city. The area was so saturated with snipers that I had to install the satellite system on the rooftop of a skyscraper by wearing my Kevlar vest and helmet and low-crawling to put the parts together in pitch-black darkness.

That's one of the more surreal experiences of my life. Back then, contractors were allowed to travel with weapons. I never left the International Zone without my MP5 machine gun and Iraqi 9mm pistol. It was a wild time. We even had grenades for protection in the villa where we lived.

After successfully working in this position for six months, I was promoted to Afghanistan site lead. In this role, I managed all satellite systems for the organization in Afghanistan.

* * *

It was a big move up, but I knew it was just the first step. During my initial week on the job with Proactive, CEO Marc LeGare visited our headquarters while he was in the country meeting with government VIPs. Marc was a retired Army colonel and a West Point graduate. I used that visit to ask him what type of education I needed to join the management ranks. He told me that as a young man I should get a bachelor's degree and likely a master's to be competitive.

I took his advice and enrolled in college while in Baghdad. It's important to note that back in 2006, the only university I knew that had PDF textbooks was University of Phoenix. Online school was a fairly new concept then, and most schools that offered online programs mailed books through the post office. Because I was in a combat zone, I ran the risk of not getting my books on time. I couldn't take that chance.

In addition to its online format and PDF books, University of Phoenix offered a wide variety of IT programs. So, I set off to get my bachelor's degree in IT and eventually my master's in business.

Although I knew a bachelor's degree would allow me to qualify for more management positions, I had to meet certain labor category requirements for jobs that worked with different technologies. For example, to work on Cisco routers on the government network while I was in Afghanistan, I needed a CCNA certification. I couldn't get authorized without it. When I was stateside and trying to improve my skill set, I enrolled in a five-day CCNA boot camp in Sacramento. I passed the exam and became a Cisco Certified Network Associate. I then enrolled in three iDirect satellite systems classes to improve my satellite systems knowledge and get certified in the satellite systems technology I was working on.

My point here is that, even in pursuing higher education, I knew I would have to supplement my education with very specific boot camps. If I wanted to be the most reliable and qualified guy in the game, I had to invest in learning.

* * *

By that point, I had gone through significant challenges and transitions, from my years as a troubled teenager to my military service to becoming a government contractor. Each time, balancing my needs and desires was a delicate process, especially when I factored in considerations like money, power, and personal growth. Even as a 26-year-old, I recognized that money and power have their roles but are not the only indicators of success.

When I took the contractor position, I had to reflect on my core values. I knew deep down that the contractor role would provide me with a high enough salary that I could support my family back home in California. This would make me the patriarch or leader in my family, not by virtue of my age (I wasn't the oldest by any stretch) or sex but because of my commitment and capability. You'll recall that I almost felt like it was my destiny to follow my grandmother's example and become the go-to person for family needs. No one in our family had completed college at that point. If I were making more money, I could help a few cousins obtain higher education and give them a running start in life. I wanted to be able to do that. The contractor position supported that value for me.

I also had goals to travel the world, advance to a position of prominence in my career, and learn valuable skills that would afford me financial freedom. Financial stability was important to my long-term vision. After spending so many years as a soldier and not being well compensated for it, I felt like gaining that compensation made the sacrifice of returning to a combat zone worthwhile.

All in all, making the career change to work as a contractor allowed me to align my values (taking care of and leading my family) with my goals (progressing professionally and financially). It wasn't an impulsive choice. It was a mindful decision based on long-term goals rather than short-term financial gain.

* * *

Formulating a plan to change my life after the military involved setting clear goals and systematically mapping out the steps I needed to complete to achieve them. Every time a leader gave me high-level guidance and advice, I would listen and implement it. After I spoke with Marc LeGare in 2006, for example, I made a plan to get my bachelor's and master's degrees within three years.

I had a vision for my life that included being a top-level executive one day. As time went on, I would break down my goals into manageable steps.

Take IT. I knew after consulting with seasoned executive leaders that the key to climbing the IT corporate ladder was to continue completing new certifications. The credentials would lead to promotions and more responsibility. Earning degrees, meanwhile, translated to better earning potential and job opportunities. I would spend hours researching reputable training boot camps that would lead to certifications I could use to command more money and get better IT jobs.

I was also intentional about networking. Every boot camp and degree program opened up circles of professionals whom I could get to know and share information with, and from whom I could learn about job opportunities.

For me, setting goals against timelines ensured I could accomplish what I set out to achieve. My goal was to earn one certification per year or one degree every year or so, as well as at least one promotion per year.

Promotions, however, sometimes meant changing companies. At first, I took the position in Iraq installing satellite systems. Then I was promoted to the lead position in Afghanistan. Then I took a job out of the combat zone in Kuwait that also paid more money and catered to a more prestigious client base. Then I returned to Afghanistan for a $100,000 raise and a role in management. I had to continue to adapt, adjust, and be flexible to the government contracting market as circumstances changed. Government contracts typically lasted only three years, so that meant I could be fired at any time or have to move against my wishes. I wasn't waiting on this to happen. I was going to charge the hill and create my own destiny.

* * *

Throughout this time in my life, I had to determine what needed to change versus what could stay the same, and I did this by being self-aware and willing to assess my life whenever a decision needed to be made. Sometimes that meant educating myself. Sometimes it meant getting a certification. Sometimes it meant taking a new job or working around personal relationships to include family.

Every time, I had to reflect on my current situation and determine which aspects of my life could cause dissatisfaction and stymie growth and progress. I had to prioritize changing my life from a soldier who followed orders to someone who needed to reflect on his own mental health after living at war for so long. I had to determine what my personal relationships would look like, both in terms of delaying a long-term relationship (working overseas is tough on a girlfriend or wife back home) and prioritizing the financial support of my family. I had to focus on career development in my mid-20s to chart a course in life that had momentum.

I believed one of my superpowers back then was that I was smart enough to seek consultation and guidance from the high-value mentors and trusted friends in my life. They were government-contracting business owners, CEOs of Department of Defense companies, high-ranking military officers, direct supervisors and managers, peers, and just about anyone who could give me good advice and perspective on what changes I could make that would most benefit me.

I also had to ignore the bad advice. Several people told me that I shouldn't go back overseas because it was dangerous, that I should get a lower-paying help desk job at home. I had uncles tell me to not join "the White Man's Army" because there was nothing there for me. But I knew myself, and I knew the Army. I couldn't achieve my goals making $15 to $20 an hour at home. The military had taken from me, yes, but it had also given me life-changing opportunities.

Every time I was faced with a potential opportunity or change, I evaluated the benefits based on my goals and values. If the change would lead to more happiness, well-being, and personal fulfillment, it was worth making.

A proud member of the 3rd Battalion, 7th Infantry, in Baghdad in 2005, serving in Operation Iraqi Freedom.

Nights out in Savannah were a standard part of my life while based at Fort Stewart in the early 2000s. I made the most of being single, driving a nice car, and having a steady income.

Being a satellite systems contractor in Iraq in 2006 was dangerous work. Here, I am preparing to drive to Camp Liberty in Baghdad.

CHAPTER 4

GO WHERE OTHERS HAVE GONE BEFORE

Mentorship has to be one of the least sexy words out there. But it's everywhere. It's on LinkedIn, it's in news articles—there's even a month (January) dedicated to it.

But what is mentorship? And why is it so important?

Mentors are like guides, and they can help you through all sorts of challenges. Uncle Willie was probably my first mentor. As a kid, I idolized him for his strength of character and personality. I used to follow him around family barbecues and cookouts and imitate everything he did. I just instinctively knew he represented the best of manhood.

In retrospect, I couldn't have chosen better. He was the first person to tell me that with education I could do anything in life. He only had a high school diploma, but he was one of the most intelligent people I'd ever met.

There are professional mentors too. This is usually what people mean when they talk about mentorship on networking sites or in *Forbes*.

Those mentors help you figure out your professional calling and how to get there.

I've had a lot of professional mentors over the years, as well. Marc LeGare is a perfect example. He is a religious man with impeccable principles and one of the first truly strategic thinkers I ever worked with. In some ways, I learned how to think strategically from him.

He was also the first industry executive who offered me direct mentorship and counsel. His advice to go back to college for my bachelor's and master's degrees played a huge role in my eventual transition to management. I'm glad I listened!

Marc illustrated the intangibles of mentorship too. Just being in his presence gave me a sense of the kind of person I needed to become if I wanted to be not just an executive but also a leader one day. His mentorship taught me about business strategies and leadership techniques, yes. But he also taught me about the importance of leading with heart and authenticity. He exemplified that being an executive wasn't only about climbing the corporate ladder. It was also about making a positive impact on those around you.

There's no doubt about it: I've had a lot of amazing mentors. We'll get into the specifics in a little bit. First, let's take a closer look at what mentorship can provide and how to find the right mentor.

* * *

Mentorship is a huge gift to the recipient and an equally huge responsibility on the part of the mentor. If it's going to work, you both have to commit to regular contact, open communication, and clear goals.

While mentorship can be a pathway to learning about opportunities and how to seize them, there are other advantages. These include:

Education and skills: Uncle Willie wisely pointed out many years ago that skills and knowledge drive your journey. In my case, I had mentors not only urging me to pursue education but also guiding me on how to find the right learning opportunities.

Self-awareness: Mentorship can be an opportunity to reflect on successes and failures, and distill such experiences into actionable lessons you can implement in the future.

Mindset shifts: There's nothing like getting out of your own way to discover new opportunities. Sometimes a mentor offers a fresh perspective or way of thinking that opens you up to growth and positive change.

Adaptability: My journey from combat to IT to academia to entrepreneurship highlights just how versatile a career can be. But you have to be ready to learn. All. The. Time.

Resilience and perseverance: Part of being adaptable is being resilient—you pick yourself up and dust yourself off when you fail—and having the perseverance to try again.

Leadership insights: I wanted to be a leader long before I became one. But I could become one only through example and dedicated mentorship. You can't go to school to become a leader. I mean, sure, it helps to know what you're talking about and be able to speak in front of a group. But true leadership is a way of thinking and being, and that is cultivated over time.

Okay, so mentorship is a good thing both in the here and now and for your future self. Done well, it can be about more than just showing someone the ropes and leading a mentee to opportunities. It can also provide avenues to gain skills, build confidence, and acquire the tools needed to thrive in any environment.

But how exactly do you find a mentor?

If someone lacks a strong professional network, it's tougher to identify potential mentors. Certain industries or fields might be so specialized that they lack the necessary critical mass for mentors to emerge. Or a person might live in a remote area with limited opportunities for in-person networking and therefore fewer potential mentors.

Sometimes people from underrepresented groups, such as women, people of color, or individuals with disabilities, face additional barriers in finding mentors. A lack of representation in leadership positions can make it challenging to find mentors who share similar backgrounds.

But backgrounds don't always determine the mentor. (Remember Chapter 2, "Your Background Guides You. It Doesn't Define You"?) While my journey has been all my own, I do think there are some takeaways for everyone.

I have navigated from humble beginnings to professional success, and I have been fortunate to have mentors from a multitude of backgrounds along the way. Such diversity has been inspiring, and underscores how mentorship transcends things that some people might view as barriers. What matters more than racial or cultural backgrounds is the alignment of goals and values between the mentor and mentee.

Ultimately, mentorship is a powerful tool for personal and professional growth. It can break down barriers and create opportunities for success. It can foster a sense of shared purpose and mutual support. The trick is to find mentors who believe in your potential, regardless of your background, and who are willing to invest their time and wisdom in helping you achieve your aspirations.

This is especially true for individuals who may not know certain opportunities exist. Simply stating, "I don't have access to mentorship," doesn't mean it's true. It's crucial for those seeking mentors to demonstrate their commitment to learning and growth by exploring all possible avenues.

The college where I work has a massive mentorship program, but many students have yet to make use of it. I think part of the reason is a lack of awareness. Part of it might even be the callowness of youth: It can take a few trials and errors—and years—to recognize the value of mentorship.

If you are really committed to engaging a mentor, you can find one.

* * *

If you want to find a mentor but don't know where to start, here are some good options:

Network: Attend job fairs, university and school events, industry events, seminars, conferences, and workshops to expand your circle.

Online communities: Participate in online forums, LinkedIn groups, and social media platforms related to your field. The goal isn't clicks or likes. It's to connect with professionals who might be open to mentorship.

Cold calling: Mentees should reach out to experienced professionals they admire, even if they don't have a personal connection. Express your admiration and interest in their work, and ask if any mentorship opportunities exist.

It's important to be specific and strategic. Don't just ask, "Will you mentor me?" Have a specific goal in mind and a specific request. A busy professional is more apt to give you precious time and insight if you convince him or her that you are worth mentoring and that he or she has what you're looking for.

Professional development and training programs: Look for formal mentorship programs offered by industry associations, professional organizations, or educational institutions. You can expand this search to include professional training boot camps. Sometimes, signing up for a boot camp opens the door to asking a good instructor for mentorship.

* * *

I told you I've had a lot of mentors. They've come from all different backgrounds and during different stages of my life and career. To illustrate that breadth and diversity and to honor their role in my life, I'd like to tell you about some of them.

Gary and Sheryl Whaley

As you'll recall, Gary and Sheryl were the parents of my best friend, Sean. As Sean and I grew up together playing Little League baseball, Gary was at every game. He was the parent who would give you a ride as easily as he'd give life lessons about working hard and being honest. Gary would have man-to-man conversations with me and Sean when we were kids, which helped shaped us into who we are today.

Sheryl, meanwhile, led me to my career. Because of her, I enrolled at Heald College to get an associate degree in computer science. (She was an email and systems engineering manager.) This was the domino that set my career in motion. And I didn't know anything about the field at that time! Sheryl had the foresight to set me on a path that would become my calling.

Monty Tidwell

Monty was the best youth baseball coach in Vacaville in the '80s and '90s, and I played on his teams between the ages of 6 and 16. He is singularly responsible for teaching me the game of baseball.

I remember him telling me when I was 7 years old, "It's not the physical errors that hurt us, because you are still a young player. It's the mental ones we just can't have."

A lot of my hitting success throughout high school was also due to Monty, but he was more than a coach to me. Because I didn't have a father figure in the home until I was 13 years old, and because I didn't have a ride to most games, Monty frequently picked me up. My mom was working, my grandmother didn't have a driver's license, Uber didn't exist, and the ballparks were too far away to reach by bike. Monty must've given me a thousand rides over the years. During those rides, I got to see what the interactions between a father and son were like. I owe Monty a huge debt of gratitude.

Robert Whitfield

My stepfather, Robert, came into my life when I was 13 and he married my mother. His arrival marked the first time I had a full-time male presence in my home.

Robert was the person who challenged my excuses when I brought home a report card full of D's and F's in seventh grade. I can honestly say that if Robert did not enter my life when he did, I would surely be in prison instead of writing this book.

Having a worthy male figure in the home of a teenage boy is more important than most people can fathom. The percentage of imprisoned youth who come from fatherless homes is as high as 85%, and as many as 90% of homeless and runaway youth have no father in the home, according to statistics cited by No Longer Fatherless, a nonprofit organization in Florida that trains and matches mentors with youths. When boys reach their teenage years, they just stop listening unless a dominant male presence gets them back in line. Robert did that for me.

He also became my family, and he treated me like a son. Case in point: For $2,500 in 1997, Robert purchased the second car I would drive in high school. It was a 1989 VW Fox. It wasn't a car that would wow the girls, but it gave me steady transportation during my senior year, and I learned that if I wanted to upgrade my life and automobile, I had to work for it.

First Sergeant Michael "Maniac" Shirley

Michael was one of the most brilliant men and one of the best noncommissioned officers I've ever met. He had a PhD in aeronautical science, and he was a great man personally, but he was known as "Maniac" for good reason: He had a short temper when it came to bulls**t. If you weren't doing things the right way and you were the type of antagonizing idiot we all loved, Michael spared no effort in aggressively correcting you. We got a laugh out of watching First Sergeant Shirley go nuclear on some of our more behaviorally challenged troops.

Lance Geppert

I don't think there was a bigger influence in my career than Lance Geppert. Lance, who is the senior director of operations for a satellite communications company, hired me as a satellite systems technician and would later promote me to lead technician. This role was followed by management stints in Afghanistan, Qatar, Hawaii, and Florida. All told, I worked for Lance for nine and a half years.

For seven of those years, I was a manager who had weekly conference calls with Lance, and those interactions greatly shaped who I am as a leader. I developed numerous skills during those conversations, like communication, strategic thinking, problem-solving, networking, and time management.

Lance treated me like family. That meant he was loyal and supportive. In the roles I held during my tenure, I dealt with different government, military, and contract employee leadership and staff. You can bet I made a mistake or two. Throughout all of my learning curves, major mistakes, and flaws as a manager and leader, Lance had my back. I will be forever grateful for the love and support he showed me over those years. He is a one-of-a-kind leader and person.

Luis Castellanos

Luis was the first government civilian lead who helped me square away the quality of my professional presentations and work.

Nothing exemplifies the power of this lesson than the time I was tasked with compiling a weekly status report. I sent my first report to Luis without paying much attention to the details. It was low quality, halfheartedly reviewed, and missing information. Luis took one look at the report, stood up in his chair, and said, "You didn't even read this report before sending it to me." Then he walked out of the room in disgust.

This was one of the best things that ever happened to me. Luis was a process-driven and meticulous executive who taught me to have my ducks in a row before I sent important documents to important people. It raised my standards across the board.

Nik Hill

When I was promoted to site lead/project manager for a Department of Defense program out of Camp H. M. Smith in Hawaii, Nik was the director of business development. He took a liking to me and began giving me program manager tasks that would later provide me the opportunity to become a full-fledged DoD program manager, essentially like joining the junior executive ranks. Nik would write lengthy emails with insight to how the DoD worked from a strategic point of view of a contractor. This ultimately pushed me over the hump of being a people manager to thinking like an executive.

Rico Perez, Dave Allen, and Dave Lerche

When I earned my first program manager position, these three individuals showed me the ropes. Rico, who was a network engineering manager, and Dave Allen, who was a radio frequency engineering manager, allowed me to shadow them as I learned about international contracts management.

Dave Lerche, meanwhile, who was a former CFO, taught me my first lessons in finance. Every day I would go into his office, and it was like looking at Excel pay-per-view TV. Learning how to use financial metrics as a project manager is the hardest skill to master to make the transition to executive.

Dr. Linda de Charon

Dr. de Charon was my dissertation chair for my doctoral program. I remember her qualitative methods course. She was known as one of the challenging professors because she had high standards for the work we submitted. She was also the lead chair of the dissertation committee.

After taking Dr. de Charon's qualitative methods course, most students ran away from her. I ran toward her. I figured if I could present a dissertation she deemed worthy, getting past the other chairs would be a breeze. I asked her to be my dissertation chair and she accepted.

I would later go on to present my dissertation's oral defense in front of 90 first-year doctoral students as an example of how to do it. It went well and I passed, but her mentorship held one more surprise for me: She gave me the idea to apply to multiple online universities for a professorship. I did this successfully in 2018 after I completed my doctoral degree at University of Phoenix and took a part-time position with St. Petersburg College in Florida.

Eric Guerrazzi

In August 2018 Eric gave me my first opportunity to become a director of DoD programs. To date, Eric, who owned the multimillion-dollar organization I currently work for, has been one of the most influential mentors and leaders I've had the pleasure of working for and with. He's the type of person who can see strategic business moves two or three steps ahead of everyone else. No wonder my executive career really took off after Eric hired and mentored me.

Two funny stories illustrate the kind of mentor he was. The first happened after Eric announced his retirement from his company. He introduced me to the incoming president, Aaron Brosnan, by saying, "Meet Patrick. He is your director of programs, and he is getting a million-dollar education shoved up his ass one nickel at a time." All I could think was that was my life's best compliment. I was learning how to be an executive by running a company as it doubled in size for three years in a row. I knew this experience would be life-changing.

The other story happened about a year after working for Eric. He recommended that I join Vistage Executive Coaching because he knew I was a lot like him and could potentially become the company president someday. Basically, Vistage is the top executive coaching organization in the world with chapters in just about every major city around the world. Eric told me, "When you read the description for joining Vistage, don't be intimidated. You are every bit as good as any of the participants who will be in those groups. With everything you have experienced here, they will likely be learning from you."

It's funny how small the world is. About 20 years prior to Eric's recommendation that I join Vistage Executive Coaching, he had a mentorship chair named Cindy Hesterman, who was a former CFO for a large corporation. (A mentorship chair is a dedicated coach who meets with you monthly to create a career development strategy.) When I submitted my application for Vistage, I was asked who had recommended me. I put down Eric's name. Vistage then paired me with Cindy as my personal Vistage mentor. Can you imagine that? My company's owner and general manager had an executive coach 20 years earlier, and I ended up with the same coach. Almost a handoff of the baton from the great things Eric accomplished in his career to the next generation of talent. (More on Cindy later.)

Aaron Brosnan

I can safely say that Aaron is the best industry executive president I have seen in my Department of Defense career of more than 20 years. You don't meet people every day who used to be fighter pilots in the Navy, have degrees in engineering and business, and are pretty much an expert in fields such as finance, program management, business development, engineering, and operations.

Working for Aaron has given me the chance to observe how a company president can manage a growing company through challenges with a demanding customer base. Sometimes the best way to learn how to become a president is to work for one and watch how they operate. By getting a close-up view of this executive's impeccable performance, I've been able to learn exactly what is required.

For the record, it's a lot. To be a president, you have to be 100% dedicated to the organization's mission, even on your days off. In fact, you have no days off. You are responsible for everything from the physical building to employee morale, from the legal concerns to HR. It's a 360-degree approach to a job, and it's not for the faint of heart.

Lori Desiato

Lori is a senior financial director and a wonderful friend with a big heart whom I was able to work with for more than five years at a multimillion-dollar company. The open peer–mentor relationship I shared with Lori gave me executive-level insight into the financial metrics needed to run an organization, including capital expenditures, gross margin, revenue, and EBITDA. It's one thing to look up a definition, but it's another to put everything into practice and understand how each component affects an organization's financial health. She has truly been a great friend and mentor, and I'm blessed to have worked with her as long as I have.

Cindy Hesterman

Vistage was one of the best professional experiences of my life. A fundamental part of the program is having a monthly one-on-one meeting with your Vistage chair. As my Vistage chair, Cindy was able to get past the noise of my always-on mind to help me home in on what I really wanted to do with my life and improve my overall performance as an executive.

I have ideas running through my mind all the time, from new startup businesses and opportunities to ways I can improve my performance at my current job. Cindy never got distracted. I always joke that she could stare into my soul and ask me questions that I could not BS my way out of. She forced me to take a hard look in the mirror and be honest about what I was and wasn't doing correctly at my job.

Cindy helped me improve as a vice president and executive. She also helped me flesh out the idea to start my own career-coaching and mentoring company, which is my passion. I feel like I have saved myself 10 years of mistakes because of the mentorship and tutelage I received from Cindy. My time with her changed my life and way of thinking.

Bernice Whitfield

Finally, there is my mother, Bernice Whitfield. Although she isn't familiar with satellite communications and IT, she is good at strategically positioning to take the next best opportunity. She's also been a sounding board for my career decisions, whether it was to go back to Iraq as a contractor or take the director role at my current company.

Every time I said I couldn't do something, she was there to say that I could and how easy it would be as long as I tried. It feels like she channeled her dreams for success into opportunities for me, cheering me on every step of the way. I owe her a lot for what she has done for me.

*   *   *

Through the wild journey of my life, mentorship has emerged as the golden thread that tied everything together. This collective group of mentors (as well as others I haven't mentioned here) was instrumental in shaping my path, but they did much more than merely offer guidance. They provided me with the tools, insights, and unwavering support that fueled my transformation.

As a wayward teenager, I lacked direction and purpose. It was mentors (my mother, Robert, Monty, and Gary and Sheryl) who first saw the flicker of potential within me. They believed in my capacity to rise above my circumstances, and they offered me guidance, patience, and a steady hand to navigate the turbulent waters of adolescence. Through their mentorship, I discovered discipline, resilience, and the power of setting goals.

In the Army, I found myself surrounded by mentors who were not only seasoned soldiers but also compassionate leaders. They taught me the importance of camaraderie, the value of teamwork, and the indomitable spirit that arises when you know you have someone watching your back. Their mentorship instilled in me a sense of duty, honor, and determination to carry on in the face of adversity.

Transitioning from military service, I embarked on a new chapter as a satellite technician in a combat zone. There, I encountered mentors from various fields, each contributing a unique perspective to my growth. From technical skills to leadership insights, they imparted wisdom that was invaluable in navigating the corporate world.

As I ascended the corporate ladder, I continued to seek out mentors who had walked the path I aspired to tread. They were the beacons guiding me through the complexities of corporate culture and leadership. They helped me develop a strategic vision, hone my decision-making abilities, and understand the nuances of effective management.

Mentorship did not end there. As I pursued higher education and became a college professor, I discovered the transformative power of mentorship from the other side. I saw firsthand the profound impact that guidance and encouragement could have on students seeking their own paths. I was reminded that mentorship is not a one-way street; it's a reciprocal relationship in which both mentor and mentee stand to gain and grow.

Finally, my entrepreneurial journey was marked by mentors who shared their experiences of building and scaling businesses. Their insights were instrumental in my overcoming challenges, seizing opportunities, and nurturing innovation.

The big picture of mentorship is this: It's a bridge between potential and achievement, a catalyst for personal and professional growth. It's the embodiment of the concept of standing on the shoulders of giants. Mentorship teaches us that success is not a solitary endeavor but a collaboration. It is the universal key that unlocks doors, transforms lives, and paves the way for countless success stories, each as unique and inspiring as the last.

**My Uncle Willie Horton was one of the
great influences on my life.**

**Coach Monty Tidwell (far right, back row) was another
major influence on me. With my mom working, he gave
me countless rides to practices, times during which I
benefited from our "father and son" conversations.**

I lived and breathed baseball, although the glove was bigger than my head.

CHAPTER 5

FAMILY AND OTHER CONSIDERATIONS

Mentorships like the ones I described in Chapter 4 are integral to professional success. On the flip side of that relationship coin are the personal connections that make life worth living and, in many ways, inspire people to work hard and achieve success (whatever that may look like for each person).

In my case, I've had lots of relationships. I had my mom and stepfather, my best friends, my mentors, my colleagues—plenty of people who've supported me and whom I supported in return. But the fact is I've never had that one, long-term personal relationship that eventually led to marriage and family.

Throughout life I knew on some level that a serious relationship would have required me to put down roots in one place and with one person, which would've restricted the freedom I needed to reach my full potential both professionally and personally. I've had to make real-time career decisions every few years, which often required me to move to different cities, states, and countries at a moment's notice. I've essentially had to build the plane as I flew it, so to speak.

The traditional family unit was the price I paid to achieve my dreams. It wasn't a conscious choice but one I made over the course of decades and countless smaller decisions in which I prioritized my career and advancement. Here's how it unfolded.

* * *

When it comes to dating and relationships, you could say I arrived to the party a little late. I found myself on the periphery of the dating scene in high school. The girl I always wanted seemed elusive. So did most of the girls at the top of the social pyramid. It wasn't like I didn't date at all; it was just that I never quite made the connection I yearned for.

I'm not sure why. Maybe it was because I was shy around girls. Maybe it was because I was into baseball instead of basketball or football. Maybe it was the way I dressed or the fact that the best-looking guys in the school were my best friends, and I got lost in the shadows.

Now, dating in high school isn't the same as dating in the adult world. Character, leadership, and potential are qualities that adults generally value in relationships. In high school, on the other hand, it's usually about social status and good looks.

This could be because we don't teach our kids better. Or it could be that high schoolers are still kids and they're dating in a microcosm where long-term relationships aren't really on the radar. As a result, they date casually and frequently based on whom they're attracted to. It's a definitely skewed experience. The problem is that it can leave a long-term impact. For me, those years were marked by an ache for love and relationships that influenced my dating life as an adult.

On some level, my high school experience suggested to me that I wouldn't find lasting love in this country and culture. Men tend to be risk-versus-reward calculators. I didn't want to spend my life chasing the approval and affection of people who didn't like me for who I was.

As I grew up, I learned that the path to love and relationships is not a straight line but a winding road with unexpected turns. I met incredible women who saw the real me, beyond the adolescent insecurities and teenage awkwardness, and I found them while I was traveling the world.

I didn't set out with this objective in mind. But in looking for meaningful connections while prioritizing my career, I experienced a series of profound relationships that gave me the sort of validation and insight I craved, even if they didn't result in the traditional happy ending of marriage and family.

So, how did all this come about? With, ironically, an immature outlook.

When I was 26, I was working as an overseas government contractor. I was locked down on military bases in Baghdad for 10 or 11 months out of the year and would get three two-week vacations during that time. To travel back to the U.S. from Baghdad, you had to stop in Dubai, Qatar, or Kuwait. This ended up being an opportunity to live a no-strings-attached kind of lifestyle.

*　*　*

If you were a 26-year-old man living in a combat zone for months at a time with no contact with the outside world, and you were given a three-week vacation with a pocket full of money, what would you do? I'll tell you what I did. I traveled the world, and I loved every minute of it. It was a combination of dangerous living, exploring new countries, meeting beautiful women, being introduced to fine dining and luxury travel, exuding the aura of a three-time combat vet who was the baddest man on the planet, and being the patriarch of my family to whom everyone came for resources and advice. Oh, and while all this was happening, I was reaching new heights in my career.

It was an amazing time I don't regret. In fact, I would recommend it to any man in his 20s who seeks adventure and change. In sports, a free agent is an athlete who is about to hit the open market and can court the best offers from multiple teams. This approach in a lifestyle context results in the same "best offers," but in terms of both relationships *and* careers. No one owns you, professionally or romantically, so if people don't respect or appreciate you, you can always search for greener pastures.

I've seen it before: People treat those who lack skills or experience the worst. If you're an overseas tech with no real credentials, for example, your bosses can treat you horribly because where else are you going to go to make that kind of money? As a contractor and even in the military, I have worked for bad leadership, and I vowed never to be held down for lack of accomplishment. Instead, I committed myself to building so much personal value through education, certification, and experience that I would always have professional flexibility.

After serving in three combat tours, I wasn't about to let anyone else tell me what I was and wasn't going to do. I called the shots in my life then, and I do now. You should too. I'd rather jump off a cliff myself than have someone push me. You should always have your best interest in mind. Your employer may or may not. The loyalty of the game only applies to the player, never the owner.

Romantically, this approach calls for a similarly singular mindset. There's no marriage, no long-term relationships, no living together, because all of that could slow down your career. This appealed to me in my early 20s because I'd lost faith in relationships. After watching marriages fall apart in the military (multiple deployments will do that) and my own lack of romantic fulfillment in my young life, I decided my career and environment were not conducive to a long-term romantic commitment.

Over time, this would evolve. I'd achieve a certain level of professional success and "settle down" into a series of monogamous relationships. But I never fully committed to marriage and children. While part of me mourns that absence, I also recognize the personal growth that came from this lifestyle. I had the freedom to explore different types of love and relationships, and I gained wisdom from them.

Maintaining my romantic freedom also protected me from toxic relationships and, if I'm honest, the risks of divorce. Divorce rates are high, and the outcomes aren't always fair. I respect and value marriage as an institution, but in evaluating risk over reward in every one of my relationships, I was never able to justify what could happen if "things didn't work out."

*   *   *

Traveling for love, relationships, and entertainment was surreal. I would start a two- or three-week vacation at the Bur Dubai, then hop a flight to Amsterdam, and then fly down to Rio de Janeiro before landing in Memphis to see my mom.

Or I would hang out in Doha, Qatar, and then head to Bangkok and Manila before spending time with family and friends in Sacramento.

In California I would show up at Sean Whaley's house and basically turn it into a Dr. Dre pool party from the '90s. I would stock his fridge with drinks, steaks, and seafood. He would work the grill, we would invite friends and family over, and we'd party for an entire week.

Maybe on some level these parties were my way of making up for what I felt like I didn't get to experience in high school. You tell me what psychological roadblock I was living by going overboard, and I'll tell you, "Yup, that and anything else you can think of."

I dated the most beautiful women in the world in my mid- to late 20s. A Moroccan beauty who lived in Dubai and worked for Emirates airlines. A French woman who worked for Qatar Airways who would later give me the nickname "Gigolo." It was a great time to be alive.

What I would tell any young man in his late teens and early 20s is that even if life sucks now—if you're depressed and your career hasn't taken off yet—be patient. It's greater later for men! If you focus on your purpose, build your career, and take care of yourself emotionally and physically, your best years will start at 30. You need 10 to 12 years to accomplish some goals and start working toward bigger ones.

It's wild how it works. I get hit on by more 20-year-old women now that I'm 43 than I ever did in my 20s and 30s. For me, it's because I'm at the top of my game when it comes to both wisdom and knowledge. My career and finances are on point. And I am confident because I had to earn my position in life by fighting like hell.

*　*　*

When I was 33 years old, I moved to Doha for work as a contractor. It was my second and final time working in a combat zone in Afghanistan, and I lived in an 6,000-square-foot luxury villa with four other contractors. (I was based in Qatar, but our military customers were in Afghanistan.)

The day I arrived on-site, there was a party with a bunch of schoolteachers from the U.K., industry service workers from the Philippines, Qatar Airways cabin crews from all over the world, a few people from Ethiopia and the U.S., and a few local Qataris.

Doha was an amazing place. I was there while they were preparing to host the World Cup and watched the stadiums start to go up. Dining was just behind Dubai and very similar with regard to rules. Liquor could be sold only inside a hotel or at a Qatar Distribution Center for foreigners. This meant that the best restaurants, clubs, spas, and activities were at the W hotel, Hilton, Marriott, InterContinental, and Hyatt.

Our villa became the go-to address for house parties since we all made good money and could afford to host. We had a good relationship of work and play there, and I dated a lot. The best time in my life was hanging out with what I called the "French Mafia." That was the group of roughly 20 French cabin crew women who were friends with my girlfriend, Celine. (I have changed the names of the women I write about in this chapter.) The French are hilarious with their aggressive humor. I can remember Celine telling me at the time, "Gigolo, there are three things wrong with you. One, you are military. Two, you are American. And three, you are Black. But I still love you!"

I always think about what would've happened if I had married her. She wanted me to move with her to Bordeaux and, later, Barcelona and have children with her. I wasn't ready at the time. I was still young in my management career, and I didn't know if I could make enough money to support a family at the level I wanted to. I was also living with four guys at the time, and I knew I'd have to up and move at a moment's notice.

The prospect of living in Europe with Celine and raising a family was extremely attractive. But there were too many unknowns for me at the time to make it happen.

After seeing that I wasn't ready to commit, Celine was offered a position with a private jet company that catered to Saudi Arabian royalty. She took the job and moved to Saudi Arabia. Three months later, she was in a horrific dune buggy accident that almost took her life. She lost a lung, broke five or six bones, and never fully recovered. In my soul I always feel guilty. Had I told her to stay in Qatar with me, that never would have happened to her. While I know I didn't cause her accident directly, I carry the grief that it happened or that maybe I could've changed it. It saddens me that a person so good had to go through something so tragic. Life isn't fair sometimes.

* * *

Many years later, in April 2015, I was living in Hawaii and working as an IT project manager. I hadn't been in a serious relationship since Celine, and I wasn't really looking for one. But then I met Akari.

I was playing around on a dating app, and I matched with an attractive woman. I figured, "Hey, I got nothing going on this weekend. Nothing wrong with going on a date." I invited her to a popular sushi restaurant in Honolulu, which had the best oysters on the island.

After she accepted, I drove over to meet her at her apartment, which ended up being just five or six blocks from my own. To my surprise, the woman who walked outside was not the person from the photo. (To protect her privacy among her friends, she'd used someone else's picture.) She was a bombshell—tan, Japanese—and I nearly fell in love at first sight. Over dinner, she explained that her family owned a pottery business back in Osaka and that they had sent her to America to attend an English school so she could come back and help run the family business.

Akari and I had a whirlwind love affair over the next four months. I fell hard for her. I can list all the things I loved about her—her etiquette, her gentility, her musicality, her heart of gold—but none of that captures the essence of who she was. I just felt this magnetic pull to be with her all the time.

At dinner one night with her and two of my friends, the food arrived and, not thinking about it, I kept talking with my friends. After a short time passed, and no one started eating, she lightly asked in the sweetest voice, "Is it okay if I eat?" OMG! I suddenly realized she was waiting for me to eat before she ate. This was part of her culture, yes, but it also drove home for me how selfless she was. In the back of my mind I was thinking, *She is the one.*

Akari and I did all of the cheesy touristy stuff while we got to know each other. We went to Turtle Beach, did a luau, and went out with friends. She took care of me at home, and I took care of her by making sure she didn't want for anything. We had an amazing time together.

Then, three months into dating Akari, I got a call from my director asking if I would be interested in taking a program manager job in Tampa. Do I take the job? And, if I do, do I ask Akari to go with me even though we'd only known each other for three months?

Akari wanted to have my children. She told me that nothing in this world would honor her more than to have my children. It made me feel valued; in some ways, she offered what I'd always thought I wanted.

But the other part of me, that risk-versus-reward professional, was worried. I had always taken every promotion I was offered, and it was a strategy that had worked out so far. If any of those hadn't panned out, however, I knew I could always step back and work as a field tech overseas. This promotion was different. It was essentially an executive job, and it would be my first. I struggled with what is now known as impostor syndrome. Was I smart enough? Capable enough? These jobs are serious, and you can be fired at any moment for any reason. I didn't want to risk having it blow up while Akari was there to suffer the fallout. I needed to focus on my career.

In the end, I decided to go solo to Tampa. Akari eventually returned to Japan, and I saw her only once more, when she visited me in Florida. She came to get a ring on that trip, but I wasn't ready to give it to her. To this day, I wonder if I made the right call not asking her to join me in Tampa.

* * *

If you had told me 10 years ago that Medellín, Colombia, would become one of the top South American destinations for holidays and lifestyle, I would have laughed you out of the room. Brazil, Mexico, the Dominican Republic, or even Argentina—maybe. But, as it turned out, the City of Eternal Spring stole my heart.

Medellín reminds me of a cross between San Francisco in its glory days and Singapore. Its temperate climate, rolling hills, and bright lights make it feel like a city that was simply dropped in the middle of the jungle. The only thing more beautiful than the skyline view is the Colombian women. I have never seen a larger concentration of gorgeous women in one place in my life. I've heard rumors that part of the reason for this stems from the old Pablo Escobar days when, if you wanted to get a boyfriend who was part of that circle, you had to become the most beautiful woman. As a result, women engaged in a veritable arms race of fitness, beauty, fashion, cosmetic surgery, and culture to become the most desirable girlfriend. I can remember walking by KFC in Medellín, looking behind the counter and thinking three or four of the women there could be on the cover of *Cosmopolitan*.

The fact that Venezuela, which is almost a failed state, neighbors Colombia may also impact the culture of beauty and relationships. Venezuela regularly features prominently in beauty pageants like Miss World, and with its government and economy in shambles, a lot of people have fled to Colombia. So, when you walk around Medellín, it's almost like a city of beautiful people. Don't believe me? Go to Miami International Airport at 10 a.m. on a Friday and look at the gates for flights to Medellín. Guaranteed, 50% of the flight is single men from Western countries.

And I'm one of them. It was in Medellín that I met Isabella. She was from the coast of Colombia next to Cartagena, and she stole my heart.

After dating in the U.S. during high school and my early military contractor days, I'd grown skeptical of the potential for a real relationship. But when I arrived in Tampa, I gave it another shot. And I was roundly disappointed. To give you an idea of what that experience was like, I went on at least three first dates with women who asked outright if I'd pay their rent for the month.

So, when I met Isabella—she was a college student and a manager at an American-style sports bar I frequented in Colombia—I was pleasantly surprised by how opposite of that culture she was. There is a saying in Colombia that there is no dating hookup culture. After your second date, you have a girlfriend. They are all about love, relationships, and family.

Isabella is like all of that and more. She comes from a farm town where she was raised by her grandmother. Her relationship with her grandmother and her dedication to her family reminds me of my own familial dynamic. Because she works hard, she appreciates the value of everything, big or little, the way I do. We have a lot in common.

No one has treated me better than Isabella. To give you an example, when we started dating, we would meet at the Marriott before going out to dinner, sightseeing, and just enjoying each other's company. I would show up at our hotel room from the airport, where I would find Isabella waiting for me. She would take my luggage, unpack my things, run a bath or shower, bring me a beer, and allow me to unpack my laptop to do a little work before we started out the weekend. It made me feel like I was in heaven.

Isabella has been my greatest love to date, but it's complicated. I respect her values and who she is as a person. But we live in different countries, and taking it to the next step of marriage is something I'm still not ready for.

* * *

In this chapter, I have reflected on what I call my nomadic heart, because I have faced a recurring question throughout my life: How do I balance love and freedom, commitment and wanderlust?

In general, I am satisfied with the path I've walked. I've achieved success in my career, enjoyed the freedom to explore the world, and dated remarkable women from different cultures. These experiences have enriched my life in ways that few others can claim, the most notable of which being the wisdom I've gained about what a good relationship looks like (and to never settle for less).

I am grateful to have lived life to the fullest in terms of exploration, adventure, and professional growth. I embraced opportunities instead of predictability or, worse, fear, which often holds people back. This is something I take great pride in.

But my path carries with it certain regrets. I don't have children. I never fully committed to one woman, and so I cannot know what fulfillment I traded in there for the many other fulfilling relationships I had.

I believe that it's important to acknowledge these regrets as a natural part of life. Regrets often stem from the choices we make at different points in our journey, and they can serve as powerful teachers for the future. While I may wonder what life could have been like with children, it's essential that I remember my choices have also led to an abundance of unique experiences and opportunities.

And that, in the end, is what life is all about. You start off with infinite choices. As you make decisions, pursue opportunities, and get to know certain people and not others, your choices become narrower. Could I marry Isabella tomorrow? Yes. Do I want to? No.

That's not because I don't love her. But I don't love the choice of marriage and commitment, at least not at this point in my life. The time to have taken that leap of faith feels like it came and went 10 years ago (or more!).

Today, I have the answer to the desire for connection and fulfillment that I experienced so profoundly in high school and throughout my life. I'm happy. I'm happy where I am and who I'm with. Most importantly, I'm happy with whom I've become.

With my best friends upon graduation from Vanden High School in 1998 in Vacaville. I managed to graduate, though my life—and dreams of a baseball career—unraveled that year.

I love to travel the world. This was taken in Amman, Jordan, in 2014.

Another important figure in my life was my stepfather, Robert, whom my mother married when I was 14. To pursue my goals, I paid a price in that I never achieved a traditional family unit.

CHAPTER 6

LIFE AND WORK AS A BLACK MAN

During the '80s and '90s, a disturbing narrative emerged about Black men. We were aggressive, undisciplined, and almost always prison-bound. We were destined to have children we couldn't or wouldn't stick around to raise. We were at best a liability; at worst a threat to society.

At least that's how the story went.

A lot of forces were behind this depiction. Some of it was rooted in truth—I grew up in the Bay Area during that time and witnessed the gang violence, drugs, and promiscuity that plagued our community—but much of it was also hype. And that hype created a stigma that I carried with me both consciously and unconsciously throughout my life.

In some ways, that stigma pushed me to do more and do better. I made it a point to present an image that countered the stereotype. It was crucial for me to come across as professional, upstanding, and caring; to embody qualities that challenged the notion that African American men were undisciplined or criminal-minded. I understood on some level that my actions and demeanor could create a counternarrative and offer evidence that one's character and performance transcended race.

What I've learned in the intervening years may surprise some people. I've had the privilege of being a part of a generational transformation that has propelled more people of color into positions of influence. My journey to becoming a Black executive has taught me that opportunity is available for anyone who is willing to work for it. In some ways, being Black was actually an advantage: I received tutelage from people who didn't look like me but wanted to see a person of color succeed.

If you had asked me if this were likely when I was 17, I would've said, "Absolutely not." But at 43, I can say that, likely or not, it was my personal experience.

*   *   *

As a disclaimer, I can only speak for my experiences and those I witnessed. I'm not naive to the fact that discrimination has and does take place based on someone's gender, race, culture, or even ideology. But while I have experienced discrimination in my life, I have experienced far more support.

My executive upbringing, so to speak, started in the military. There, First Sergeant Gilpin, a Black man from the Bahamas, used to tell me and other Black soldiers, "You aren't Black. You are Army green. No one in the Army cares about what color you are. All we care about is if you can do your job. Do you operate with the Army's core values of integrity, selflessness, and honesty? If you are injured on the battlefield, do you care what color the person coming to save you is?"

During my time in the military, we never discussed race. We were all Americans. If you behaved like a proud member of the armed forces, you could be counted on. If you were selfish or lacked integrity, you were deemed a "blue falcon" no one could trust. (In military slang, the "b" and "f" originally stood for a profane phrase that essentially meant betrayal.)

While character trumped everything else, I did notice that most commissioned officers were white and more noncommissioned officers were people of color. I suspect this was primarily because to become a commissioned officer you needed a bachelor's degree. Of course, you could get that degree after serving in the military, so that course was open to me. In addition, I received powerful mentorship in the military. White commissioned officers who were captains and majors noticed that I was a smart noncommissioned officer, and they took opportunities to share their knowledge about how military leadership and strategy worked in their ranks.

Fast-forward to my civilian career in 2011 when I was an entry-level project manager on the government-funded Internet Café Program under Lance Geppert. Lance is a white man from South Dakota who went out of his way to mentor me (see Chapter 4). He had weekly calls with his overseas managers to provide them with guidance on meeting company objectives. Normal calls would last 30 minutes. With me, Lance would stay on the phone one to two hours over our allotted time. He would ask me about my life and what my goals were, give me strategic insights on how to handle difficult employees in the workplace, and guide me on how to carry myself with pride and dignity at the executive level. When I would meet with other project managers who were white and mention these impromptu lessons, they would say, "He only has a 15-to-20-minute sync with me and then we end the call!"

I could tell that Lance knew the history and perception of young Black men, and he took pride in doing something good to help move a young, hardworking kid along his journey. It was a symbiotic relationship: He perceived me as needing more help, and because I was willing to listen and learn, he took the time to give it.

Or how about Marc LeGare, the CEO of Proactive Communications in 2006? I was a lowly field technician, and he pulled me aside and gave me a fully triangulated case for why I needed to get a master's degree if I wanted to be in management and achieve long-term success in the field of IT and DoD contracting. He was a white West Point graduate from California. He was also devoutly religious and spent hours talking to me about life and what it means to be a good person who helps others. He wanted to give back in any way he could.

I've been fortunate to encounter many individuals along my journey who saw beyond the color of my skin to my potential. And who actually put pen to paper and gave me a shot to succeed in life. When I delivered, they gave me more and more opportunities.

Many people offered me extra attention and tutelage, not because they pitied me, but because they genuinely wanted to see a young, positive, hardworking Black man succeed. This support bolstered my confidence and served as a reminder that, as much as some racial disparities may persist in certain aspects of society, there are many individuals who are eager to uplift those willing to put in the work.

Having grown up in the aftermath of the Civil Rights era, I understand the propensity to mistrust. Someone shows you bad behavior for decades, and you should believe what you see. But when people make an attempt to change, you need to let them change.

As a 17-year-old, I was told to not trust white people. And I believe a lot of other African Americans were offered the same advice, probably because the people offering it had had their own negative experiences. But when you see representation over and over again within a community of people who want to help you, what should you trust? Your lying eye?

Of course, there have been instances when I have seen people from less culturally diverse backgrounds shy away from me because of their ignorance. But all in all, I have seen more people invest themselves in my success than not.

What would I look like telling you white people were bad, when throughout my life white families have fed me, clothed me, given me rides to baseball games and amusement parks, praised me for how smart I was, purposely sought me out to give me guidance, and facilitated my fair competition for jobs?

No one cares about your color, culture, race, or feelings as a man. They only care about your performance! If you can execute, they will hand you the baseball and tell you to strike this MFer out in the bottom of the ninth with two outs, bases loaded, and up by one run. I know, as a Black man, I'm supposed to carry the flag of race baiting. But I'm tired, old and grumpy, and I can only share my truth. We live in the legacy of Dr. Martin Luther King Jr., where we all have the opportunity to become anything we want. No more excuses. Put in the work and get it done, or try harder and smarter the next time.

Here's why I feel this way.

* * *

Growing up in a suburban school, I was privileged to learn early on how understanding a multitude of cultures would enrich my life. In many ways, I got to live in the center of the melting pot that America proudly described itself as being.

Not that I saw it that way back then. But having best friends who were of a different race exposed me to the diversity of the world early on. I learned to appreciate the different experiences inherent to other cultures.

These seeds were planted early on, but they were not without their weeds, which presented mostly as conflicting narratives. On the one hand, I had best friends whose families treated me like their own. I mixed with other kids from different backgrounds in school without issue.

On the other hand, I had family from rural Mississippi, Tennessee, and Chicago, and the stories coming from them painted a picture of a world where diversity was not always celebrated. Some family members shared stories of extreme racism they experienced in the past. But because progress had been made in such a short time, I found myself not being able to map those negative experiences to what I was experiencing. My lived experiences early on helped me develop a more inclusive perspective.

I also had a different background. While my biological father wasn't in the picture, Uncle Willie was and, by the time I was 14, so was my stepfather, Robert. Their guidance and support played a crucial role in shaping my work ethic, aspirations, and my sense of place in the world. Uncle Willie grew up working on a farm in Mississippi. He used to tell me how he was driving tractors at 7 years old and working on the farm or around town as soon as he was able to walk and be productive. Robert worked full time as the athletic director at a California state prison, but he also had a knack for parenting (he's the one who called my bluff about my poor grades) and an amazing DIY skill set. One summer I watched him build our entire backyard, from pouring concrete to building a deck, fence, and canopy. He even planted the grass and garden. These two men exemplified the value of hard work and commitment to family.

I saw the other side of Black life too. Leroy (my cousin who came to live with my mom and me for a little while) lived that side of the coin. His experience served as a cautionary tale for me precisely because our lives and backgrounds were so similar.

Leroy and I were raised in a middle-class neighborhood. After high school, the world beckoned Leroy with the promise of opportunity. He'd seen how being honest could have negative ramifications. (You'll remember how his honesty regarding marijuana use had potentially cost him a job with the state prison.) What he didn't know was that the world at large would be just as unforgiving.

Like many young people who lack proper guidance, Leroy ventured into the unknown seeking who he was as a person. He encountered temptation in the form of women, drugs, and alcohol. This path led him to connect with people who indulged unchecked in these vices. But there was one problem. Those other people came from wealthy families with safety nets.

At first this didn't matter. But over time Leroy found himself making one unfortunate decision after another with regard to drug and alcohol use. The feelings of freedom and excitement that accompanied those initial decisions in youth didn't age well, especially with his humble background.

Why did I bring up money? Because the fate of Leroy's affluent friends looked a lot different from his. Those kids had bail money and lawyers hired by their parents. Those kids had therapists and rehab.

We all love a story of an underdog who makes good in life. Well, it's as heartbreaking to see the opposite: financially strapped kids who essentially destroy their lives with a few bad choices made between the ages of 18 and 22. The stakes are so high, and these "adults" don't even know it.

As Leroy resurfaced when I was a young adult going through challenges, the undeniable truth weighed on me. Wealth has the ability to protect people from life's consequences when they make a few mistakes. My cousin didn't have that luxury. Leroy's life, like those of many other financially challenged kids, was devoured by the system.

Leroy and I are in a sense the same person. But where Leroy decided to venture out on his own in a world that swallowed him whole, I decided to venture into hard work and education.

I idolized Leroy, and his devastating trajectory taught me something valuable. His failure was always front and center in my mind as I grew up. It helped reinforce the importance of discipline and work. It helped steer me away from drugs and other negative behavior. It acted as a sort of boundary line for my life that I knew I could never cross or I might suffer the consequences he did.

Today I sit here as a vice president, college professor, business owner, and author. The key differences in our situations, the variables that pushed Leroy in one direction and me in another, were minimal. I had the benefit of a mother and, by the time I was 13, a stepfather in the home. I changed my grades from 3 F's, 3 D's, and a C to a 3.0 in two years. I saw what could happen to my life if I lived down to the expectation society had for Black men. I learned that the road to success in life is not always equal. Second chances like the one I got don't always present themselves. You have to know when to take them—and count yourself lucky.

*   *   *

Ultimately, I believe that my experiences didn't limit me but pushed me forward. Seeing my uncle and stepfather work hard, and witnessing the consequences of Leroy's life, made me buy into the adult system early on and prevented me from making a bunch of destructive mistakes in my 20s.

Once I was in the military, it didn't take long for me to figure out I wanted more than the life of a combat soldier or an IT support specialist. I had ambition and, thanks to my mentors, I had a pathway to achieving it.

I also carried the right mindset. I came of age as things were beginning to change. It takes time to heal old wounds, and the generations that preceded me gave me advice based on their lived experiences. Nothing in this world is perfect, and there is more work to do regarding race relations, but I believe that the progress preceding generations made put me in a position to be the primary determining factor of success or failure in my life.

How empowering is that? Instead of asking myself whether race relations were perfect, the question I tried to answer as a Black man starting his career in the 2000s was whether I had a fair shot at making it. The answer was an unequivocal yes.

Why waste energy worrying about whether race relations could be improved? My time was better spent focusing on what I could control and building upon that. As it turned out, I was able to control a lot.

No one has ever denied me an opportunity or job because I was Black, but I did bear a subtle burden as I worked my way up. I felt a responsibility to prove that I could achieve success through hard work and dedication, just like anyone else. I don't know if this burden was self-imposed or imprinted on me because of my family history, but it drove me to strive for excellence and validation.

There are universal themes in life, no matter your race. Those themes are work, success, and the importance of connections and social circles. I believe that emphasizing them is what has allowed me to celebrate and learn from other cultures rather than fear them. My experiences with youth sports, the military, trade schools and university, travel, food, and co-working have enriched my life and broadened my perspective.

* * *

Being different often meant I had to find a balance between being true to myself and conforming to workplace norms that may have felt foreign to me. It meant adapting to corporate cultures that were sometimes at odds with my authentic self, all in the name of making those around me feel comfortable and challenging their preconceived notions about who I was as a Black man. Over time this made me exceptionally adaptable. It also shaped my belief that we must meet people where they are so that we can establish the best connections possible.

Don't get me wrong: Codeswitching isn't always easy, especially early in life. As a young executive, this tension and linguistic filtering can feel taxing. I sometimes felt the need to suppress elements of my authentic self, such as verbal expressions that could appear slightly aggressive to people outside of Black neighborhoods. (The kind of talk I'd hear in a barbershop, in other words, is not what I'd engage in at a corporate office.)

For Black executives, this might feel as though you are not being true to your identity. I also don't think there is anything inherently bad here. I don't speak for all Black people by any means, so bear with me. I didn't grow up boating, fishing, camping, golfing, and participating in a host of other activities that most people who come from a predominantly white culture do.

A corporate environment has the expectation of a certain level of conformity to these predominately white standards of activities, behavior, and communication. That can involve a learning curve for someone who comes from a different culture. To me, that's just the spice of life. You have to be willing to explore and try new things and take it in stride.

Because I've had to navigate between different professional, cultural, and social contexts throughout my life, I've developed an intellectual flexibility. It's a skill that many people of color are familiar with, and it has been instrumental in my journey, allowing me to connect with a broader range of individuals, gain valuable insights, and make amazing connections, all while furthering my career.

* * *

The flexibility that accompanies codeswitching and adapting to other cultures ties into another Black advantage: resiliency.

Think about it this way: Part of the foundation of the Black American experience is rising through adversity and recognizing that, in regard to education and career, we often have both a responsibility and an opportunity to be the first in our own families or social circles to reach new heights in life. I believe this show of determination can influence others in your circle to want to strive for more instead of just doing the bare minimum of showing up to work every day.

On many occasions, I've been able to influence others through my unwavering desire for self-improvement. When I was a satellite technician with the Internet Café Program in Afghanistan, everyone steered away from management roles. The prevailing attitude was that the drama and stress weren't worth it.

When I arrived I told management that I wanted any promotions they could offer me. I said that I wanted to be in management one day and that I'd do anything to get there. Once I went public with my quest for management, others began to voice the same. And when the people around me learned that my grandmother had only a third-grade education, that I was essentially two generations away from sharecropping, they understood my desire and began to see the logic in it. This made them see the pride and opportunity inherent to seeking promotion.

Another example is when I started getting certifications while I was staffed in Qatar. I did this so that I could qualify for other management positions. The technicians who worked for me began getting industry certifications as well because they suddenly saw through me the value in achieving those credentials.

Beyond that, I have had countless employees and peers who decided to go back to school for associate degrees, bachelor's degrees, master's degrees, and even doctorates because they saw what education allowed me to achieve.

I also made a point of career coaching my employees over the years. I'd advise them to stay in functional positions in their early IT careers for only two to three years so that they could build the necessary experience to become an executive one day. They saw how

I was able to gain momentum in my career because I wasn't afraid to work hard, learn, and adapt. And they wanted to do the same.

* * *

In the 1980s, 1990s, and early 2000s, Black communities were very family-oriented, despite what you saw in the media. Everywhere I've gone in my career, I've been able to foster a similar sense of family and community within the teams I've led or been a part of. I've been able to cultivate a strong support system and inspire our teams to be part of a greater mission than just our individual selves.

When all else fails, there's always the food. In 2022 my company had a potluck Thanksgiving lunch, and my mom made enough food to feed almost 80 people. Everything from collard greens to sweet potato pies, baked chicken, macaroni and cheese, and honey-baked ham were on the menu. Black culture—and the virtues of sharing and connecting through food—is one more thing I've brought to the workplace over the years. I like to think that has touched everyone at least a little.

Ultimately, I believe one of my biggest contributions is serving as a role model and trailblazer. I believe the more executives out there who look like me, the more we demonstrate to young people that reaching the highest level in your career is possible if you put in the work. You don't have to play sports or be in entertainment, and there is no longer a glass ceiling. Black communities have always been resilient. Now we have access to the opportunity and mindset that can help us transform our narrative for the better.

The men in my family who taught me what it means to be a stand-up citizen. I'm fourth from the left.

CHAPTER 7

KNOW WHAT YOU WANT AND GO FOR IT

If race weren't holding me back in my career (and in my case, it wasn't), and if education were attainable over the course of my career (and in my case, it was), then there really was nothing I couldn't achieve. I just had to have the mental clarity to know what I wanted and the drive to get it.

That sounds easy enough, right? But sometimes knowing what you want is the hardest part. And if it's not, knowing *how* to get what you want is.

* * *

Find your purpose. Get clarity. Know your mission.

There's no shortage of phrases out there encouraging people to have a game plan when it comes to their lives and prioritizing goals, all of which just goes to show you how common and widespread this phenomenon of coasting through life is. If everyone lived with purpose, there wouldn't be so many books, programs, and coaches offering to help you find it.

In some ways, finding what you want boils down to who you are. This crystallized for me when I faced that bully on the bus in seventh grade. That encounter was the moment I chose between a life of fight or flight. It was the seed that grew to reveal how important it is to know what you want and be willing to go after it in the face of adversity.

Oddly enough, in that moment on the bus I just wanted peace. I guess when you are a young boy without a father, you feel alone in the world. I had Uncle Willie, who filled a tremendous void. But I didn't come home to my father every night and have those basics— like learning how and when to stick up for yourself—ingrained in me. I didn't want to fight that bully that day. I just wanted the situation to go away. As I would find out over and over again, some battles in life must be fought. And if I had to fight, I wasn't about to lose.

This was the start of a long path in terms of figuring out what I wanted. The determination had been there, latent, all along. Figuring out my direction and goals started the day I refused to be bossed or bullied.

Every setback I had to fight through and recover from, and every success I experienced, got me closer to clarity. Excelling in baseball, completing my associate degree, passing basic training—each of these experiences allowed me to build the confidence I needed to become a man who could unapologetically call his own shots in life.

The Army was a major proving ground, in fact. I believe the Army taught me that true confidence is attained through accomplishment. It's not just blind belief in yourself, which can be delusional. It's waking up every day and getting those small wins so you know that, if you can complete one task today, you can complete the next task tomorrow.

In the Army you might complete an obstacle course by crawling across a tightrope 50 feet in the air one day. Another day you might learn the basics of being a rifleman or how to march correctly or how to read a map. It's a series of steps that culminate in becoming a basic combat soldier.

I believe that confidence through accomplishment exists in us all. We all have the ability to find ourselves, particularly when we are young and devote ourselves to the things that interest us, whether that's sports, performing arts, writing, or learning a strategic game like chess. Anywhere we get to experience healthy competition so that we can practice self-improvement results in accomplishment. Once you have an opportunity to succeed in life through your own merit, you can discover who you are and who you want to be.

This is why I advise young people to find their purpose through participation. Life happens outside! You have to get out there and compete. The only guaranteed failure you have in life is when you don't try. It's important to learn the skill of effort, failure, and success early in life when the stakes are low so that when life throws you a serious setback, you have the experience and mental fortitude to handle it.

* * *

There's another situation to consider as well. In life, you may find yourself in the trailblazer position. Being the first to do something in your family or social circle, whether it's going to college or starting a company, can be exhilarating but can also open you up to disapproval and even hostility. Believe me, I know. Every major decision throughout my life, such as joining the military or starting my own company, has been met with at least one detractor.

Being able to withstand cynics and critics can be a superpower in the right circumstances. If you have a passion and a skill for something, a dream you have to chase, or a role you feel you were meant to fill, you gotta do it even if no one understands why. You owe it to yourself, and doing so will help you build the confidence and courage to do more difficult things later on. This can lead to successes in life that others can't achieve because they are afraid to try. Become comfortable with the hate, the criticism, and the challenge to your position, and you can accomplish anything in this world.

This reminds me of something I learned when I managed the Internet Café Program. It was November 2011 and the executive lead for the Space and Naval Warfare Systems Command walked into my office. He informed me that the current country manager, my boss, was being fired (for inappropriate behavior, no less), and he asked if I were interested in taking over as the country manager of the 50-person combat zone program. I would be responsible for making decisions that could affect the safety and lives of my contractor employees who traveled day and night around Afghanistan installing free satellite systems for troops.

I told him, yes, I would be honored to be the country manager but pointed out there was a previous deputy country manager who had stepped aside only because of the trouble with the recently fired country manager. I didn't want to step on any toes.

The executive lead (Luis Castellanos) turned, looked me in the eye, and said, "Power isn't given. It's taken!"

It turned out he had approached the other manager for whom I was more than willing to step aside, but that manager said he wasn't sure if he wanted the extra stress and responsibility. This was an immediate turnoff for the big-time executive who was looking for a leader. He wanted someone who was all in.

I can't tell you how many qualified people I know who take the attitude of "If management wants to give it to me, I'll let them ask me." This is counterproductive. You have to tell people you want a promotion. You have to then demonstrate your desire by improving yourself through education, certification, and experience. Once you broaden your knowledge base and skill set, you can raise your hand and compete when the time comes. And if you don't succeed, try again harder and smarter next time.

If you are going to live the life, you need to lead the life.

Are you all in? Are you ready to grab opportunity when it shows up? Are you ready to own your destiny?

* * *

The idea that power is taken rather than given encompasses the reality that influence and authority are not willingly ceded. You will be actively challenged by leadership, peers, and subordinates, all of whom will want to seize at least a little power to achieve their own goals.

Now, when I reference power, I'm referring to the individuals whom we choose to follow. These are the people among us whom we trust to make decisions regarding our policies, affairs, and actions. These people should be the most experienced and ethical in your group.

The person in power should also have the most technical expertise, knowledge, and skills for the domain in which you are working. This will allow him or her to properly influence the team from a position of competence. If you are not this person and you are still in training, you need to understand your position and limitations and seek opportunities for improvement until you mature into someone capable of responsible power.

Do you lead with a set of core values and consider fairness when governing? Do you have the ability to self-reflect to ensure your desires for governing are about the greater good of the team and not yourself? Lastly, do you take responsibility for any consequences that your actions as a leader may have?

When I decided to take over the Internet Café Program, I had:

- More combat experience than any of the 50 contractors in Afghanistan on my team
- The highest technical skill set of a satellite technician in the program
- Infantry experience (unlike most communications experts), which mattered since ethics were one of the most important traits a person could display on the battlefield

I had also demonstrated management-level communication, leadership, empathy, and the ability to inspire others to do the job because they had watched me do it successfully.

I didn't take power because I smelled weakness. I took power because I owed it to myself and my team to lead them successfully.

* * *

There's a phrase I often rely on when talking about the trajectory of my career: You can't run with the wolves at night if you spend all day running with the puppies.

There are no breaks, in other words, when it comes to determination. You can't sit in your parents' basement playing video games for five years and then expect to get rich and retire early. You have to find the fire within you, and then you have to consistently nurture and refine it.

Life gives you plenty of opportunity to do so. As I mentioned, I've been fighting for survival my whole life, from the trenches of the battlefield to the "battles" in the boardroom (where sometimes tens of millions of dollars and a hundred different jobs are on the line).

What's interesting is how I grew into this person. If I were to describe myself, I would tell you I was the kid who got beat up so much by life that I became tough. I wasn't born with value. I had to create it, and I instinctively knew that success had to be achieved one step at a time. That would take endurance.

This is good news for most people. You don't have to be the best, smartest, or most talented to succeed. You just have to have vision and grit.

For example, when I entered Heald College to get my associate degree in computer science, I quickly realized that everyone else was way smarter than I was. My overwhelming brilliance wasn't going to win me any awards because I didn't have any. The people in my classes had been working with technology and electronics since childhood, which meant my only advantage was the work ethic that my family had instilled in me.

I can remember getting 400-page books in AC/DC electronics, semiconductors, transistor-transistor logic, digital electronics, and computer hardware and software design and not having a clue what any of it was about. I didn't know how to program a computer or how to build electronic circuits.

What I did have was time. While most students would skim the chapter summaries and then take the exams, I would read all 400 pages in each book. I would leave school on Friday evening, get home, and read from that moment until Monday morning. I'd read every chapter and every word (even the glossary) of every book so that I could give myself the greatest opportunity to understand these complex subjects. It wasn't easy and I struggled. I didn't have any money to go out and party, but I had the drive to study and try to become proficient at each subject.

Graduating from Heald with my Certified Electronics Technician Certificate and Associate of Applied Science in Computer Science was revelatory. Before I started that program, computer science was as foreign to me as Mandarin. By accomplishing that program, though, I realized that if I put my mind to any subject this world had to offer, I could learn it. I was never going to be the smartest guy in the room but with enough hard work, I could close the gap.

I carried this mentality with me as my career went on. In the military I couldn't shoot. I wasn't the best soldier. I didn't have the top physical fitness score. I wasn't even the best communications soldier, which was my job function. What I was was hardworking. I came in undisciplined and unskilled, but in a short time I was able to work myself into a position of prominence.

When I became a contractor in 2006 I knew nothing about satellite systems or computer networking. Conventional knowledge would tell you I was destined to be a low-level IT tech for the rest of my career, because I didn't have a degree, and I didn't have skills or knowledge about satellite communications. (Most people who enter jobs like that never improve themselves. They're making executive-level money and don't see the need to learn more and advance their careers.) I quickly identified every industry certification of relevance in my field, and I got to work completing them. I had the clarity to know I wanted more, and I had the determination to go for it.

I was also smart enough to know that I would never be as technical as Bill Gates, even if I took technical courses for a thousand years. I knew that I needed to diversify, so I went back to college and began working on my bachelor's degree. With that, I thought, it wouldn't matter if I couldn't do all of the technical work because my responsibility would be to find the people who could. I'd be the manager; they'd work for me.

My motto has always been to stay two steps ahead of the competition. When everyone was getting a bachelor's degree, I went and got a master's and then a doctorate. When people were getting the Project Management Professional® (PMP) certification, I went and got PgMP® (Program Management Professional) and PfMP ® (Portfolio Management) certifications as well. When people were happy with their overseas tech jobs earning $200,000 a year with a Level 1 skill set, I decided to become the lead tech, then manager, then executive because you never know when a tech position will get cut. I didn't plan on waiting around to become obsolete. I wanted to keep pushing the limits to gain additional job security and see how far I could go. I wanted to be on top.

When everyone got comfortable working their 9-to-5 jobs to retirement with only 401(k)s to live off of, I saw inflation coming. I decided to diversify my earnings portfolio by taking an adjunct professorship on the side and then create an LLC to see if that could yield extra income. That way, if I were fired from my day job, I would still have money coming in.

As you can see, my whole life has been about the opposite of living at the mercy of other people's decisions. That means being strategic and looking ahead. That means working harder than anyone else.

My goal was never to outwork others for a season or a year or even a few years. I wanted to outwork everyone else for as long as I was in the game. And when they caught up, I had to have enough vision and determination to move the goalpost and keep working.

I am not an alpha, overconfident person who walks around bragging about all that I can do. Nor am I of the opinion that it's enough to simply think happy thoughts and "manifest" success.

In fact, I would say that my mind can be quite chaotic. When staring down the barrel of the massive PMP exam—and failing it twice—I felt like maybe I wasn't good enough to pass it. I took my own advice and worked smarter, not harder. Instead of doing more of what I'd done (unsuccessfully) before, I enlisted in a boot camp to learn about the exam from a professional. I had to spend money to make money, and I had to recognize there was a better way to do something than I originally thought. This was a serious learning moment for me.

When I told my mom I would try for my doctorate, I couched it in all kinds of disclaimers that essentially amounted to saying I wasn't sure if I could do it. I'd encountered so many people who'd gone through the program only to give up, ABD (all but dissertation). I didn't want to fall into that category, so I needed to research the program, understand what it was about, and build a game plan to complete it.

Every job I've been promoted to I had impostor syndrome: *I'm not sure I'm good enough to be here. I may fail and get sent back to where I came from.* Those voices have accompanied every step I've taken in life.

Those doubts are also accompanied by adrenaline, the kind that likely sees a fighter through to victory. And the fear keeps you humble. It forces you to identify possible negative outcomes and, to conquer them, create a plan of action with milestones. This is exactly what I have been doing for 20-plus years.

I pick a new adventure, think of the ways I could fail at it, and then slowly and methodically create a plan to overcome and attack the mission. It's almost funny, because on those occasions when I've been overconfident and thought positive thoughts like, "I'm so smart, I'm so brilliant, this is going to work because I believe in myself," I've failed miserably. Not because I couldn't do it, but because I didn't see the obstacles clearly and practically or my strengths and limitations.

When I was a newly minted manager for the Internet Café Program, I didn't review metrics or come prepared with answers to meetings. I thought I could wing it or charm my way through those meetings, but I just ended up looking stupid. A few experiences like that, and I soon realized that anytime I was cocky about something, I would get humbled real fast.

When I get the knots and butterflies in my stomach, I am ultimately successful. It's a physical signal to me that I'm nervous because I need to do it, and I don't know if I can. That, in turn, creates the laser focus I need to succeed.

Success, after all, is like luck: It boils down to clarity and determination.

As a young boy, hanging out and searching for my way in life...

...and the man I would become. Operation Iraqi Freedom in 2005.

CHAPTER 8

IN CHARACTER

When I see men dancing on TikTok, it tells me all I need to know.

Now, I realize TikTok is a softball and, yes, I'm taking the shot. But I'm doing so for more than a laugh. To me, TikTok is a symptom of a culture in distress.

For example, there was a viral trend at one point called the "Go White Boy Go Dance." Essentially, a beat drops and someone starts an awkward, goofy routine. As the beat speeds up, so does the dancing and (for the viewer, presumably) the mockery.

On its surface, it's harmless. Entertaining even. But the message gives me pause because I think it reflects a wider trend: Men don't have to be strong, serious-minded, principled or ready to lead. They just have to be willing to let others laugh at them. They have to be harmless.

I grew up striving to be the opposite. I wanted to become the kind of man who was strong, led by his convictions, and able to remain calm under stress. I wanted to be a force for good. How can rising generations acquire those skills when they get up every day with the purpose of performing for others? Of generating likes, shares, and comments? How does that dopamine hit (and subsequent striving for dopamine hits) impact a person's convictions, motivations, and overall behavior?

I know I wouldn't want to go onto the battlefield—or into a boardroom for that matter—with someone who was more concerned with optics than substance.

It's not good for society or co-workers, but it's not good for men either. If you encourage the world to view you as laughable, it doesn't take long before you internalize that perception. What is the emotional toll of building your persona, brand, and life on being a joke?

There's a well-known quote by the writer G. Michael Hopf that goes: "Hard times create strong men. Strong men create good times. Good times create weak men. And, weak men create hard times." We've experienced the good times. We're on what comes after that.

More and more, I see men who appear unable to cope with a changing and challenging world. They respond by getting depressed, getting angry, or getting out of the U.S. to someplace with a slower pace. I don't have all the answers as to why. I just know that this trend isn't good for us and that what we're doing isn't working.

Our current cultural climate impacts men and women alike, of course, and some of what I have to say can apply to both sexes. But as a man who has lived through four decades of varying personal and global experiences, I feel positioned to speak to young men specifically. I have gone to war as a private in the Army, succeeded as an executive in the business world, and taught in academia. I have lived pre- and post-internet. I have started my own company. I've earned a seat at the table with an informed opinion that I hope will help others. So, please read on with that in mind.

In the preceding chapter, I talked about the nature of power and going after what you want. This chapter adds more nuanced context to that advice, because power only works for the greater (and the personal) good when it comes from a place of integrity. I believe that young men have an opportunity to reshape and redefine the idea of good character. But first they have to develop a solid understanding of character itself.

* * *

For anyone like me who served in the armed forces, developing character was easy. We had no choice but to operate with honor and integrity. If we didn't, we got isolated or flushed out. When another soldier demonstrated untrustworthy behavior, like gossiping or being envious, or did something without the best interest of the group at heart, the group would ostracize him. Depending on the nature of the infraction, soldiers could even be discharged for "behavior unbecoming of a noncommissioned or commissioned officer."

Promotion, meanwhile, meant living by the Army's core values of loyalty, duty, respect, selflessness, honor, integrity, and personal courage.

Transitioning back into civilian life, many of us found ourselves with an intangible competitive edge: It seemed character was (and is increasingly) in short supply.

Take, for example, my career when I was 26 and out of the Army. I was working for a company with government contracts, and I behaved accordingly. If I said I'd be someplace at a certain time to deliver a product, I was there to deliver it. If the product had an issue, the customer didn't have to come looking for me. I searched them out to provide honest answers.

My character, in other words, made me a reliable and standout employee. So, when the opportunity arose for me to take over a

$100 million program as a country manager, my organization didn't hesitate to give me the reins even though I was only 31.

I continue to define good character based on those principles of resilience, ethical decision-making, integrity, and a sense of duty to something greater than myself. But I find myself in the minority here. What happened to all the stoic men? I don't mean the toxic version of stoicism, the kind that catapults men to the top of the food chain at the expense of everyone else. I mean a practice-based way of living that lets you focus on what you can control in life. You can be kind and caring to others. You can have a sense of duty and pride to protect and provide for your family. You can embrace an attitude of never giving up.

Being stoic, in my mind, means you don't crumble the minute you encounter adversity. You stay calm, remember your training, and make good decisions. You take a rational approach to solving problems.

Think of it this way: Do we want the men of tomorrow becoming more and more addicted to attention, or do we want them to embrace self-discipline, levelheadedness, and being purpose-driven? That is an "emotional tool kit" that can see them—and those who depend on them—through any crisis or challenge.

There's an old country saying that seems to apply to a lot of young adults today: They have an alligator mouth and a parakeet butt. They talk a big game but are as soft as Charmin toilet paper. If every feeling isn't validated, many people don't look inward and ask themselves, "What am I doing wrong?" They don't find empathy or curiosity for the other side. Any advice to look inward is seen as gaslighting yourself. According to modern culture, it's better to project outward with shame, blame, and deflection rather than seek greater understanding.

This doesn't just happen among young people. Plenty of adults have unfortunately retreated to their respective corners of any given debate and camped out there for the long haul. But our future is in our youth, and I worry about what I see in the rising generation. Specifically, the tendency to dismiss opposing viewpoints as an emotional assault rather than an opportunity to engage, discuss, and grow. If they don't learn how to get a little uncomfortable and maybe see where the other side is coming from, what does that mean for their future? .

Well, I'm here to give it to you straight. Every competing opinion isn't an assault on you personally. Engaging in healthy, informed debate is a cornerstone of American society. Done right, it can lead to real progress like civil rights, improving quality of life, and making our country one that continues to afford opportunity to all of its citizens.

I recently saw a townhall-style interview with commentator Candace Owens. One of her audience interactions came from a student who said she felt actively victimized by Owens's presence on the campus. Owens's response was, "Life's tough. Get a helmet."

Now, you may or may not agree with Owens's politics, and that's okay. It's also okay to debate the substance of an issue and to do so with vigor. But to lead off with what the late YouTube personality Kevin Samuels coined as S.I.G.N. language (shame, insults, guilt, and the need to be right) is not respectful or productive. More importantly, it's not okay to take that approach with someone who is older and more accomplished than you are. Where does that stop? Should we be okay with 20-year-olds calling 70-year-olds names? We need to return decency and respect to the American lexicon.

* * *

How did we get here?

It's normal for young people to rebel and agitate for change. But the zeitgeist that has more young people rejecting everything (and everyone) that came before can't be good for society any more than it's good for relationships and personal fulfillment.

Whether the cause is bad parenting, social media, identity politics, politicized education, or a combination of all that and then some, I can't say. All I can say is what I said earlier: What's happening now isn't working.

On social media, I sometimes feel like we give the microphone to the loudest and dumbest people out there because sensationalism sells. TikTok and Instagram have their place to allow young people to display their talent and creativity and be their authentic selves. But I think that the technology has moved so fast that we haven't properly set boundaries and guidelines for young men and women to follow.

We have a weak, microwavable culture in the U.S. There's no love or care put into the meal that is our culture. Just put it in the microwave and press "start." Then, when a new fad comes onto the scene, toss out the old and sit down to whatever the latest, cheapest microwavable meal is.

Again, this comes back to character. Entertainment is fine, but life is more than entertainment. Debate is fine, but culture and legislation must be hashed out through informed debate, not talking points culled from Instagram memes and outraged TikTokkers.

This isn't just the musing of a Gen X man. Look around, and you'll see how this lack of character plays out in the big picture all across the country. Consider, for example, Los Angeles, San Francisco, Chicago, Minneapolis, Philadelphia, or New York City. Do you want to move there? Do you feel safe there?

People fail to realize that society's problems—rampant homelessness, rising crime, substance abuse—isn't about money. It's about values. You can pour $1B into San Francisco, Chicago, LA, and New York, and it won't fix a thing. You have to invest in character and values.

Right now, that's not happening. It used to be that even if people lacked resources, they didn't just walk into an Apple store and start stealing iPhones. It used to be that people could organize marches or protests without devolving into rioting and looting. Theft wasn't reframed as reparations for past wrongs. Righteous anger, as during the civil rights movement, motivated real but peaceful change, not the terrorization of city streets, toxic environments online, or the rejection of all tradition because some of it wasn't working. I believe that part of regaining our character as a society and rebuilding a collective ethos is to reintroduce stoicism to men. Ethical decision-making, seeking virtue, committing to hard work, and never giving up—cultivating these qualities in ourselves is the first step toward remediating some of the challenges in our society.

I have seen this work in the Army, which trains troops to operate ethically while carrying out a range of duties. They aren't told, "Do this," or, "Do that," for no reason. Rather, they are imbued with a set of core standards that unifies them and gives them a sense of purpose when carrying out orders. Whether they are executing a combat mission or refueling tanks, every soldier understands that their work contributes to the whole and is vital for overall success.

If we take that approach as a country, our society will be better prepared not only to interact with each other on a day-to-day basis but to face future, as-yet-unknown challenges as well. We live in an era of constant technological change, where the unprecedented advent of artificial intelligence is coinciding with the interconnectedness made possible by social media. That translates to a nearly unfiltered exchange of information where people are forced to face moral dilemmas daily. We will be better able to address those dilemmas if we have built a society that is resilient, committed to doing the right thing, and unafraid of hard work when it benefits everyone involved. That is the value and the power of a collective ethos.

*   *   *

The importance of character is also paramount in the workplace. My own experience illustrates this in a variety of ways. People want to work with me and they want me to run their programs, because I have integrity and discipline. I present myself as a resource to their mission, so they seek me out. I tell them that my default answer is yes and that I will do anything in my power to support their mission. I promote young people in my department, so I have a reputation for being a leader who looks out for his people. I am known as the program fixer and the problem solver. When I'm around, things get better. That's why I've been offered the most prestigious jobs all over the world managing hundreds of millions of dollars.

On the flip side, I've seen how a lack of character in the workplace can wreak havoc on a team. For example:

- I've seen managers engage in illicit relationships with government sponsors, placing the contractor company business (as well as the government reputation) at risk.
- I've seen childish and aggressive behavior kill future business opportunities.
- I've seen leaders treat employees like servants to the detriment of both team morale and company reputation.
- I've seen company leadership scam the government and lose out on competing for future contracts.

- I've seen leaders intentionally filter information to executive leadership because they're afraid to give bad news or look incompetent.
- I've seen executives usher in a culture of purposeful sabotage so they look good at the expense of other department heads or employees.

Lack of character, in other words, can destroy organizations just as it can society.

* * *

Changing a society begins with you. If you can't stomach an opinion that's different from your own, you need to get over yourself as master of the universe and start focusing on real things that matter in our society. I'm talking about strengthening families, improving education, and restoring balance to a country where it's far too easy to cancel or sue someone you disagree with.

From there, you have to build your emotional maturity. One major lesson I recommend to young men is to make a conscious effort to practice empathy, self-reflection, and mindfulness. Having a sense of introspection when dealing with others goes a long way to seeing why people hold the opinions they do.

For example, I've been in relationships with women from all over the world and who have very different personalities and expectations. I never approached these relationships from a position where I sought to dominate the other person. I didn't want someone who'd blindly follow me anywhere or who would give in the minute we disagreed. I wanted someone I could learn from and who could learn from me. What if we approached all relationships—romantic, platonic, and professional—with emotional maturity?

Being curious and careful with other people—even when they say something you don't like—will allow you to develop other positive character traits too. It helps build emotional intelligence and just regular intelligence. You don't know everything. Sometimes other people can teach you things. But you can't hear them if you're arguing aggressively or using shaming language. That shuts down any ability to mediate with others because no one gets heard.

I think that this can help us to redefine masculinity in a more positive and impactful way. It's good for men to protect and provide for their families, friends, and community. It's good for them to be resilient, discerning, independent, and thoughtful as people and leaders. The toxic attributes, like inflexible thinking, aggression, misogyny, and emotional repression can go. Those don't help anyone, and progress is vital to propel our society forward.

As you work to listen more and talk less, to be uncomfortable when someone says something you disagree with rather than trying to shut them up, look for role models. Find someone who lives this way, and align yourself with him or her. Look to military service members, law enforcement officers, blue- and white-collar professionals, and anyone who works in a position where integrity is part of the job. There, you just might find examples of the character you seek. (And check out *The Leader's Companion* by J. Thomas Wren.)

Always form your relationships based on mutual respect and trust. If you base them on quid pro quo in regard to money or status, those bonds probably won't last. Always remember to practice accountability for your actions, and continue to lead and grow as a person. Becoming a lifelong student means you gain perspective and wisdom while you give discernment, integrity, hard work, and loyalty to those around you. That's how you change your life—and the world.

CHAPTER 9

LEADERSHIP (IT'S MORE THAN A BUZZWORD)

"Sometimes in life you need to mow the lawn to see the snakes."

My mom said this to me recently when I was dealing with a personal conflict, and I nearly fell out of my chair. She was right, of course, and in more ways than she knew. Life is not compartmentalized. If you have unresolved issues or problems in one area, they often spill over into other areas.

For the better part of the last 15 years, I have worked in management. When you are in management, you carry influence in multiple spheres. You impact the strategic direction of the company. You have a say in who gets promoted, hired, and fired. You set the tone for your company culture, and one unspoken truth of this responsibility is that it's good form to be generous. That applies to your knowledge *and* to hosting your employees, peers, and their associates.

In my case, I've always championed career growth and camaraderie among my employees. I push for that promotion when they deserve it. On the social scene, I'm always the first person to buy drinks at the bar, treat people to nice dinners, or share my mother's amazing cooking at the company potluck. Anyone who has worked with me knows I'm also famous for bringing in a hundred freshly baked chocolate chip cookies, banana nut muffins, or cheesecake cupcakes just because it's Monday.

This type of generosity has helped make me a well-respected and popular person. The question, however, is what happens when you stop bringing food, paying for dinners, and providing bottle service on the regular. When you pull back the benefits, who still likes you?

Throughout my life I have done this very thing. Not as a test, but in response to life's ebb and flow. Because I work in sprints, I will disappear for three or four months and bury myself in studying for a portfolio management certification. Or I'll take time to prepare for my dissertation's oral defense. Or I'll focus on developing my digital training courses or, lately, writing this book. I will not leave my apartment from Friday evening until Monday morning except to go to the gym or grab food, so I can focus on a task or project.

In this way, I've essentially mowed the lawn, and I can see how those around me respond. Does their love and admiration disappear? Do they still invite me out when they aren't sure if I'll pick up the bill?

The people who still rock with you and call to check on you when you pull back the benefits are the comrades, battle buddies, and friends you can count on. The people who become almost adversarial once the benefits disappear are the snakes my mom was referring to. If you ever question who is truly down for you, mow the lawn in your life and let people tell you who they really are with their actions, not their words.

This is important when you graduate from manager to leader, because you have to understand people in order to lead them. It is impossible to compartmentalize your personal and professional lives, because they will always intersect. That's why the most profound and effective leaders live out the principles of leadership 24/7 with everyone they encounter. Whether they be in business, politics, or academia, true leaders inspire greatness from others because they themselves strive to be great.

I came to this realization over time. Gradually, I recognized that leadership transcends acquiring degrees, certifications, and work experience or simply having managerial skills. You can't get a degree or certification in management and think, "I'm a leader now."

Rather, leadership in its most authentic form guides every action, reaction, and interaction. It's about managing your organization with your team members. It requires a level of selflessness that pushes you to place the good of the collective above your own advancement and, in the process, draw out the very best performance from those around you.

Here's a closer look at what leadership truly entails.

* * *

My responsibilities as vice president of program management for a satellite systems company primarily require me to assist the president in managing the organization's strategic project portfolio.

To operate as a VP, I need strong communication and interpersonal skills when interacting with my government customers and industry partners. I have to understand proper stakeholder management to maintain key relationships with high-profile clients. I need to understand how to manage, identify, assess, and mitigate risks associated with the programs I run. This can include funding, customer technical requirements, and political challenges. I need to have a deep understanding of financial resource allocation, budgeting, and cost-control metrics.

I also need to know when to trust my gut. How is this customer going to react when I give them bad news? Should I come with a carrot before contacting them? Maybe take them out to a steak dinner before giving them the news? Maybe this news is better coming from someone higher ranking than me. This critical-thinking process is something I've refined in my role as an executive and leader.

To me, it's part of competence in leadership, which we'll explore a little bit later. First, I think we should look at an equally important but rarely identified part of leadership: having a motivational and innovative mentality.

Being innovative isn't just for addressing KPIs and organizational strategy. It's often best applied to managing people. Think about it. Most people accept they will work from the time they are a young adult until they retire at 65. Not all of us will get to build a career on our hobbies or passions in life; many of us will simply work to live. Well, it's my job to inspire the people around me so they feel like they are living their passion. I do this by encouraging a culture of ongoing growth and improvement.

Workers who continuously improve their skills and knowledge will grow in value to the organization. These "knowledge workers" will also grow their enthusiasm for their work. Learning—and being able to use what you learn—creates a spark of creative excitement every day, because you get to do something new every day.

Imagine what it must have been like playing for the Golden State Warriors during their 2015–2022 run of excellence. In those seven years, the Warriors won four championships and went to the NBA finals six times. It's fun and exciting to come to work when you're winning. It's easy to inspire and innovate because you know there is a high probability your hard work will pay off.

Now imagine playing for a last place team. It's more difficult to come to work and get inspired when you don't have any wins to show for it. Your job as a leader would be much harder because you'd have to tap into undeveloped potential.

That's not easy to do, but one way I've found success is through cross-functional training. Basically, I ensure that my team members are available to support all departments in my organization at a moment's notice.

Often, my engineering, operations, finance, or business development departments have critical projects or deadlines but are short on staff or expertise. I encourage other department executives to request my program managers to assist with those tasks. This means my team members are not only learning program management and contract support from me, but they're also learning about engineering fundamentals, supply chain, or financial metrics and strategy. What's more, they get to practice innovation by applying their skill sets to other department missions.

Knowledge acquisition, after all, is a compounding asset. Imagine how their knowledge will grow exponentially by supporting all of these departments. Those departments, meanwhile, see my team members as value-add employees rather than deadweight or, worse, liabilities.

So, when my team comes into work each day, they have no idea what they are going to be working on. All they know is it will be exciting and they will learn.

I have used this methodology to lead in every organization I've been a part of because I'm always looking for opportunities to make my teams better. If a team member is interested in finance, I send them over to that department head to see how they can help. In this way, I create self-sufficient, accountable leaders in an environment that is exciting and steeped in learning.

I always joke with my team members that I expect them to become better VPs than I am because they got to learn from me and take my skill set to the next level. As leaders, we have an obligation to promote, mentor, and encourage the next generation. Yes, this "gets the job done," but more importantly, it evokes a sense of legacy in rising team members so that they can someday pass the baton themselves. Our goal should be to draw out every bit of potential and creativity each team member has to make them better people for work, for society, and for the next generation.

* * *

Another aspect of functional leadership is, necessarily, the right educational background.

As you know, I hold bachelor's, master's, and doctoral degrees. I also hold a number of major industry certifications, including:

- Project Management Professional (PMP)
- Program Management Professional (PgMP)
- Portfolio Management Professional (PfMP)
- Certified Information Systems Security Professional (CISSP)

I have additional experience in several other industry and nonprofit endeavors.

With all of this, I've become a college professor, a knowledge-commerce entrepreneur, and an author. I've spent a lifetime achieving my education and experience because they give me a competitive advantage in the workplace. Every job I apply for, every entrepreneurial proposal I submit, every professorship I toss my hat in the ring for, my educational credentials and experience help boost me to the top of the selection process.

That's important, but you usually need more than industry expertise to become a true leader, and that's why leadership training is so important. I believe that leadership training should be a pivotal focus in an employee's career, and it should start early.

My first major leadership training came in 2003 when I attended the Army's Platoon Leadership Development Course, which was the basic leadership course required to become an Army Sergeant Grade E-5. I didn't know it then, but that course would provide a basic leadership framework that I carry with me to this day. It made me start to look at everything through a different lens, one that centered on being responsible for people's lives and accountable for the mission at hand.

Since then, I've only expanded my understanding of leadership. In fact, I've been formally developing leadership skills for more than 20 years, and I will continue honing these skills for the rest of my life. I have taken courses, enrolled in coaching programs, and read book after book to soak up as much knowledge as I can.

My goal in learning is to provide as much value to my organization as possible while also taking a big-picture approach to my own career and goals. I decided to start my LLC while working my full-time job, for example, just so I could create an opportunity to run my own business and achieve a certain work–life balance I knew I'd want in five to 10 years. That took a certain amount of intellectual investment. Throughout this book I have emphasized that knowledge is a compounding asset. The more you learn, the more you help yourself—and others.

*   *   *

No matter how many "I Love Me" certifications and degrees adorn your office wall (and I'm guilty of this!), true leadership encompasses more than education. It hinges on cultivating greatness from your employees, developing competence in your field, and, sometimes, removing bad leadership.

Leadership is not a venture to be taken alone but should be considered a joint effort with the next generation of leaders. As I said, my goal is to be generous with my wisdom so that the next generation can take my place one day and be even better than I am.

This may or may not be popular with the old guard of leadership, but I will take it a step further and say that I even believe in letting future leaders know what I consider their unlimited potential to be.

The old-guard way is to never keep your leaders informed of what it is they truly bring to the table or how good they really are. I think the goal of this is to prevent complacency from setting in. If up-and-coming leaders think there's nothing to improve on, their performance might drop.

I think this is a huge mistake. Praise often and let individuals know they have the ability to become VP one day. As a matter of fact, I think you should say, "Here is what you should strive for, and here is a road map to achieve it."

I've seen firsthand what happens when you don't communicate openly about someone's potential. The individual may not have the vision regarding what's possible, so they aren't strategic about filling their gaps.

Earlier in my career I worked alongside a talented Microsoft engineer. He was the most adept employee in our program and had the potential to become director and vice president someday. After several years of doing his job flawlessly, he decided to shop around his résumé. He didn't see anything in his future at our current company outside of a cost-of-living salary bump or a slight merit raise. Our executives were so busy with other work that they didn't take time to map out this person's career or share the opportunities that existed for him. Only after he delivered his two-week notice did the company tell him about the potential he had to be promoted to director or VP someday. It was too late.

Keeping people dumb and blind doesn't work anymore. People want to know what the future can hold for them if they invest themselves in an organization. Good leaders recognize that and respond accordingly.

* * *

Now let's discuss the concept of leadership through competency. In the DoD contracting environment, particularly in my role, effective leadership is crucial for success. You have to be useful to the group at large, because people want to look up to you for guidance. To provide that, you have to be competent in your field of work or show some value that others can admire and benefit from.

As 50 Cent once said, you can't be a "wangster" and survive in this life. (That's a fake gangster who pretends to be someone they are not.) It's better to do the work and earn your value through accomplishments.

As a practical example, leadership in my position would include competency in various disciplines within the DoD realm. In addition to everything I outlined earlier regarding communication and innovation, I need to demonstrate an understanding of defense acquisition and contracting processes, such as knowledge of procurement regulations, contract types, and compliance requirements. I need to have technical experience and expertise in satellite systems technologies so I can make strategic decisions about organizational road maps. I need to know about strategic performance management, planning, and vision with regard to aligning my organization's mission with the evolving satellite technology road map that my customers and stakeholders want to utilize one day. I also need to have a deep understanding of quality control and assurance alongside the sustainability of the product and services I am providing. That comes with education—and experience.

I bring those competencies to the table for my organization's top brass. For those I manage, however, I bring something else. I bring that innovation and commitment to career development I mentioned earlier. I also bring a responsibility to protect them from toxic work environments.

"Sometimes the dog that bites you is the one that, if you give him a little bit more food, will get him strong enough to bite you again."

I heard this somewhere, and I believe it holds a lot of relevance in business. It's the responsibility of leaders to always remove bad management and toxic employees or risk them destroying the organization's culture.

There are many professionals in high-status roles who practice bad leadership. The dog that bites, for example, can be bad leadership that needs more than a leash to rein them in. Bad leadership in a company or department is like a cancer that must be surgically removed. When you're basically asking employees to stick with you through thick and thin, you have to return the favor by removing bad leadership if you see dysfunction. If you don't, and if you then judge the employees for leaving after a bad leader has terrorized their lives, ruined their workplace reputation, and eliminated their morale to continue in the field, then it's you who has broken the social contract.

*　*　*

As a leader, I also need to commit to inspiring a sense of legacy in my team. I've explored this theoretically, but sometimes the best way to convey something is by showing.

So, consider this example. At my company, we have a certain reputation for excellent customer relations. I've worked in positions where, when we first win the contract, I am the acting program manager for a short period. I allow younger employees to watch how I interact with the customer and essentially inform the customer that my goal is to be a resource to them. I will always be honest and transparent, and the customer can call me day or night for anything they need. My default answer is yes (to the best of my ability).

When you treat your customers in this fashion and in front of your employees, it becomes infectious and, as a result, people follow suit. It becomes the default way we treat customers both now and for the programs we win in the future. I pass the program over to the manager and, later on when he's promoted, he passes this same customer-focused and customer-first culture to the deputy project manager he's training. This is an example of how you create an ongoing legacy of quality customer service.

The legacy we leave behind from one program to the next is not just a successful execution. It is a cultural shift within the team. Done right, every team member will cultivate a sense of purpose and empowerment so that they transcend the role of employee to become the guardian of the organization's impact on the industry and their community.

In short, committing to legacy building has a multiplier effect that impacts the leaders of today *and* tomorrow. And that long-term vision is just one more characteristic of true leadership.

*   *   *

Recommended Reading

I'm not the first person to weigh in on what makes a good leader. Here are some of the books that have shaped my thinking:

Positive Intelligence, by Shirzad Chamine

Leadership to me is about teaching the tenets of what Chamine coined as Positive Intelligence (PQ), which measures the percentage of time your mind is serving you rather than sabotaging you. This book outlines the concepts of PQ and how to spend more time reaching your potential.

The Leader's Companion, by J. Thomas Wren

I referenced this book in the previous chapter, and it's a good one. Wren walks you through a collection of works by ancient and modern leaders who discuss the challenges of leadership, both in theory and in practice.

The 48 Laws of Power, by Robert Greene

Leadership to me includes recognizing which strategies your adversaries will use against you so you can combat them and protect your team. This book explores power through the ages to identify 48 enduring principles for those who seek—and seek to prevent—absolute power.

The Art of War, by Sun Tzu

There's a reason this book rings true after thousands of years. It may have been written for the Chinese military in the fifth century BC, but the strategy still applies today for professional leadership.

The Five Dysfunctions of a Team, by Patrick Lencioni

If you want a readable guide on managing people, this book identifies five behaviors that can wreak havoc on any team. It's told within a fictional framework of a new CEO taking her unruly team in hand, so it's readable and educational.

Good to Great, by Jim Collins

Looking for more research and less philosophy? Then this book, which analyzed 28 companies over five years, is the one to read for management strategy insight.

CHAPTER 10

EMBRACING THE FUTURE

Being a leader requires strategic, big-picture thinking. Well, nowhere is it more important to be a leader than in your own life. So, I challenge you: What is *your* big picture? What are *your* goals? What do *you* want?

Vistage's executive coaching taught me to make my goals big, bold, and audacious. That helped when I was growing my day-to-day career, and it also laid the groundwork for my passion project: the LLC I started called Professional Career Transformations (PCT).

PCT was born after I'd spent about two decades mentoring and guiding employees. One day in 2020 I woke up and said to myself, "There's a real gap in the market for the kind of basic career and leadership development skills that I learned from the leaders in front of me. Why hasn't anyone put together a course on the building blocks of career development and the art of career progression?"

It nagged at me enough that I brought it up during a mentoring session with my Vistage executive coach, Cindy Hesterman, now the CEO of Vistage Florida. I asked her, "Why doesn't something like Vistage exist for entry-level employees, college students, military service members, and mid-career professionals?"

She replied that a program for up-and-coming talent was in the works, but even that felt a little niche. I reflected that over the course of my career to that point I'd managed four or five programs with young professionals who had the same challenge: They didn't know how to build structure in their careers or create career advancement opportunities for themselves.

That was when I decided I would start writing down everything I'd learned, almost like a career life story, and organize it into a structured framework of my best practices. That, I figured, could at least nudge someone toward starting a conversation about career advancement and possibly begin moving in a purposeful direction with their career.

That is how I developed my two signature digital courses for the 6-Figure Career School, which lives under the PCT umbrella. (The courses are the 6-Figure Career Blueprint and Strategic Career Building.) Just as the journey through leadership is about the continuous climb rather than simply reaching the top, so too is career development about continuous learning, adapting, and progressing. My courses aim to equip individuals with tools to climb the corporate ladder while simultaneously developing a deep understanding of leadership's multifaceted nature.

Ultimately, I want people to use my life lessons, best practices, and tools as a guide to achieve their own dreams. In fact, I want them to expand on them and make them better. Nothing would make me prouder than to have someone tell me, "Dr. Horton, you recommended I use education, certification, and experience as the framework to create a career road map. I took what you did and expanded on it by adding skills, clubs, associations, and projects to make it better."

That is progress. As Tony Robbins says, "Success leaves clues. Go figure out what someone who was successful did, and model it. Improve it, but learn their steps. They have knowledge."

For me, PCT is a pathway to this advice. It wasn't just a business venture but rather the philosophy that I developed after years of mentorship by some of the world's best leaders.

In addition to the 6-Figure Career School, PCT has an eight-course module on financial literacy, plus one-on-one career coaching. For the former, I wanted to include some basics on financial literacy since some of the biggest decisions young people make coming out of high school center on financial topics, like student loans, credit card debt, and banking—topics that a lot of people, like me, never learned in school.

The coaching lets me help clients build a career road map for strategic success. That one-on-one work echoes my experience at Vistage and nods to the power of mentorship.

PCT's ethos—that knowledge acquisition is a compounding asset— informs all of these offerings. The interest you gain from lifelong learning and continuous improvement compounds over time and allows you to effect change in your life and the lives of those around you. This change happens faster and faster as you acquire and apply more knowledge.

PCT's courses allow participants to explore their resiliency and practice self-discovery in order to create a game plan for their futures. In business, you need a programmatic approach through a plan of action and milestones to achieve objectives. (We call these POA&Ms.) The same goes for life. POA&Ms create a clear path for accomplishing career goals and setting up the most joyful personal life possible.

What those goals and life look like is up to you. Mine includes making top dollar in the United States and living abroad part time in places like Latin America, Europe, Asia, and the United Arab Emirates.

* * *

In this book, I've shared with you the motivation that fueled me to accept nothing less than the best for myself. For me, it's family, redemption, and giving back to those less fortunate as so many people did for me when I was lost and as I later worked my way up the ladder. Maybe that's why, as I reflect on my life's journey, one feeling rises to the top: I feel lucky to be here.

I want you to find your own motivators. If my life story tells you anything, it should be that we all have boundless potential. We just need the right mindset and tools to harness it. We need character, clarity of vision, and mentors to help us along the way. We need determination, and we need a guide.

That's why I don't consider this chapter a conclusion but a beginning. It's part of a guidebook, a road map, and the fresh air of inspiration you might need to start your own transformation and pursue life's journey with a smile on your face.

My corporate career and entrepreneurial ventures are not independent happenings. They represent a lifetime's worth of events and experiences knitted together. Look closely, and you'll find trial and error, setbacks, and life accelerators, all of which represent a life well lived. The day I pass away (a long time from now, I hope), I want people to say, "Patrick got every mile out of those radial tires he calls walking shoes in life. He didn't leave anything on the table. He went for it, and he got it done. He lived life on his terms."

This takes courage. You need to be audacious and step out into a sometimes unforgiving world with the confidence that no matter what is thrown your way, you can navigate it. Your goal should be to emerge stronger than when you started. I want you to know that you too are lucky to be here during what is arguably the best time to be alive in the history of humanity. You should claim your independence and permit yourself to strategically pursue your dreams.

That's why this moment isn't a goodbye. In my mind, this book is a greeting. A pleasure to meet you and a call to action to determine how I can be a resource to you and support you in determining what is next for you in life. You stand at the intersection of your experiences to date and your potential for the future. Which direction will you go?

I wish I could go back in time to talk to the young Patrick Horton and let him know that although his life was tough, everything would be all right.